MOR DIRECTIONS 2

Reading, Reference & Study Skills

John Cooper

Oliver & Boyd

Introduction

The teaching of reading in the middle years involves more than the consolidation of basic decoding skills and literal comprehension. It involves also the development of more advanced skills and strategies for locating information, for using texts effectively, for critical reading, for independent study and enjoyment of print both inside and outside school. It cannot be assumed that young readers will acquire these skills fortuitously, just by reading. Our pupils deserve to be shown how to progress beyond inflexible, one-pace, line-by-line reading.

For successful reading for learning and reading for leisure, pupils need to be able to use:

> library resources, including catalogues and files;
> reference books such as dictionaries and encyclopedias;
> project resources such as topic and information books;
> "signposts" within a book, such as contents lists, indexes and headings;
> explanations and instructions such as those in textbooks, assignment cards and worksheets;
> techniques of skimming and scanning, for locating information quickly;
> context clues to deduce meanings;
> skills of inference and prediction, as in following a narrative or argument;
> evaluative processes, as in appreciating figurative language or in distinguishing between true and false, fact and opinion.

They should also be introduced systematically to the reading demands of life outside school – the special requirements of, for example, a street plan, a sketch map, a railway time-table, a pamphlet, a recipe, a newspaper, a brochure, an advertisement, a graph, chart or diagram.

The practice given in these books is not an end in itself. Assignments within the book suggest practical applications in pupils' own environments, and these reading strategies should also be applied in other everyday learning situations. In this way pupils can be helped to become more proficient and happier readers.

Much of the material in these books lends itself to oral discussion work. Sometimes understanding can be achieved more readily and with more fun when the pupils are able to discuss the tasks in groups or pairs.

N.B. It has been assumed that pupils using this book have reached at least the level of competence of *Directions 2* and can tackle this work without much further teaching of the ground-work covered in *Directions Pointer*, *Directions 1* and *Directions 2*.

Contents

Introduction

SECTION A
What Does It Say?

1. Parts of a Book

It is possible to find out quite a lot about a book very quickly.
Let us look at the three parts we may find in books.

1. What comes before the main text – cover, contents list, illustrations list, foreword
2. The main text
3. What comes after the main text – appendix, glossary, index

The Cover

Study the two examples of front covers given below.

The cover of a book tells us the title and who wrote it.
There may also be pictures from which we can draw
information.

A 1. How did policemen dress in Victorian times?
2. Name some items of equipment which they carried.
3. What do you think is happening in the picture on the
cover?
4. For which country did John Paul Jones fight?
5. Describe the type of ships he sailed in.
6. Does the picture show him as an admiral or as a pirate?
Why do you think so?
7. Why do you think there are illustrations on the cover?

Assignments

*1. Go to your class or school library. Select five books but do
not open any of them. Write out the title, author and
publisher of each one.*

Example

Title	*Author*	*Publisher*
Pirate and Admiral	Kathleen Fidler	Lutterworth Press
The Story of John Paul Jones		

---

*Where did you find the names of the publishers?
    Write down what you think one of the books might be
about before you read it. After you have read the book check
whether your predictions were correct.*

*2. Sometimes it is useful to know when a book was written. For
instance, if you are seeking information on geography, space
exploration or electronics, it may be important to know that
the information is up-to-date.*
    *All books should have a date printed on them, telling when
they were first published, plus a note of new editions or
reprints. Look for this information on the back of the title
page.*
    For one of the books chosen in Assignment 1, *make a note
of the date when it was first published, and the date of that
copy (if it is a later edition).*
    *Look also for a copyright sign (©), if the book was written
within the last 50 years. Find out what this sign means and
who owns the copyright of that particular book.*

Contents List

The title of a book and the pictures on the cover will often give you a good idea what the book is about, but sometimes it gives you a false impression. A check can be made by looking at the table of contents which usually gives us a very good indication of the subject matter.

   If the book does not have a table of contents, you might get the same information by looking quickly over the chapter headings.

   This contents table tells you the number of chapters in the book, the title of each one, and the page on which each one begins.

A   1. From which book referred to on page 4 do you think this contents table is taken?
   2. How many chapters are there in this book? (Do not count the foreword.)
   3. On which page does Chapter 6 begin?
   4. Which chapter might tell about his days as an ordinary seaman?
   5. Do you think he served in the navy or on merchant ships at first?
   6. Which chapter might tell of his greatest fame?
   7. How many pages would you read in the whole of Chapter 8?

Assignment

Go to your class or school library and select five fiction books. Does each one have a contents table? Does each contents table give you the number of each chapter, the title of the chapter and the page on which it begins? Do any of your five contents tables contain anything else?

B   Here is a contents table from an information book called *The Silicon Chip*. Not only does it give you the chapter headings but it also gives sub-headings as well. This is very helpful because it lets us know in more detail what the book is about.

To which chapter would you turn if you wished to find out about the following:
1. how the silicon chip revolution began
2. ways in which people have been helped by the silicon chip
3. what the silicon chip does for us in the home?

To which page would you turn to find out more about:
4. how a silicon chip is made
5. use of the silicon chip in cameras
6. how the silicon chip might help the blind
7. the use of the silicon chip in missiles
8. how our present money might be replaced in the future?

Contents

Illustrations List

We have seen how attractive a book becomes with good illustrations on the covers and also the kinds of information we might get from these pictures.

Inside the book there may also be illustrations to make the book more attractive and to give us a clearer idea of what is being described.

Below and opposite are parts of two illustrations lists taken from books:

A 1. From which book already mentioned do you think the first list is taken?

2. Which page would show a fire-engine used in Victorian times?

8

3. Which page would show a citizen being taken to court?
4. Which page might show a prisoner on trial?
5. Which page might show ships of the same period?
6. Which page might show what the inside of a prison looked like?
7. Which page might show the kind of reward offered by the police for information?
8. What do you think might be a suitable title for the book from which the second illustrations list is taken?
9. How do you think the sword might be delivered? (page 33)
10. From whom would they have no time to run? (page 51)

Assignment

Work in a group of two or more. Each member of the group should find a book (in school, at home or in the public library) which contains a list of illustrations. Copy down those items from the illustrations list which best show what the book is about – you may consider them all equally relevant.

See if the other members of the group can tell the main theme or title of the book from the clues given in your illustrations list.

Foreword

In the table of contents for the book *Pirate and Admiral* (page 6), you may have noticed the *Foreword* listed at the beginning.

Many books have a *Foreword* (sometimes called a *Preface* or *Introduction*).

In this short section the author, or someone else, gives us some information about the book, possibly about the author as well, and what the author is trying to do in the book.

Here are two extracts taken from introductions to books.

Foreword

There is a favourite dance at parties and balls in which ladies and gentlemen change partners each time the music changes. This dance is called *The Paul Jones*. Why does it have such an unusual name?

There was once a famous sailor, born in Scotland, who took American nationality at the outbreak of the American Revolution in 1775, when the British colonies across the Atlantic, on the eastern coasts of the country we now call The United States of America, fought to win and keep their independence from the British Crown. America had only five good-sized ships in her first navy and John Paul Jones commanded one of them and attacked British shipping. He also commanded a French squadron under the French king, Louis XVI, against Britain. Then, when the war of American Independence was over, he went as an admiral in the service of Catherine the Great, the Empress of Russia, in her war against the Turks. When Paul Jones left her service he returned to France. At that time the French Revolution was beginning, and the revolutionaries were rising up against Louis XVI and his court. Paul Jones might have become the commander of the first French Republican Navy. Indeed, this was suggested by one of the chief Revolutionary parties, but he died before he could accept. So, you see, Paul Jones changed his allegiance several times in his adventurous life.

He changed his ships many times, too, for he commanded a very great number. He even changed his name from John Paul – for Paul was his actual surname – to John Paul Jones. And because he was a man of so many changes, the change-partners dance was named after him.

He was born a very humble boy, a gardener's son on the Scottish shore of the Solway Firth, but by his own endeavours he rose to be a world-famous admiral, feared and respected by his foes, as worthy of honour for his bravery as Nelson was. He has been called The Founder of the American Navy because he captained one of the first ships in that navy. Today America looks on him as a national hero.

This book tells the story of his many adventures and battles and of his rise to fame.

Tales from a Finnish Fireside

All twenty-seven of the fairy-tales, fables, and droll stories included in this anthology from Finland have been drawn from original sources and have had in their native language the widest acclaim. Some are taken from the standard collection *Fables of the Finnish Nation*, others were told to the authors from memory by old Finnish storytellers, and all make much and varied use of the magic power of words which is unique to Finland's folklore. A strange, pastoral, peace-loving people with high ideals, a keen sense of values, a delight in the droll, and a homeland of forest and lake, emerge in an invigorating miscellany of traditional stories that has equal value as an enduring record of the Finnish culture.

11

The first extract is part of the author's introduction to *Pirate and Admiral, the Story of John Paul Jones*. The second extract comes from the introduction to *Tales from a Finnish Fireside*. Each one gives us useful and interesting information we should read before we start on the main part of the book.

A 1. Why is the dance called "The Paul Jones"?
   2. Where was John Paul Jones born?
   3. Why was he called "The Founder of the American Navy"?
   4. Why does America look on him as a national hero?
   5. What is the author setting out to do in the book about John Paul Jones?
   6. How many stories are told in *Tales from a Finnish Fireside*?
   7. Where could you read some more such stories?

Assignment

Choose five books from your class or school library. Is the introduction to each one written by the author? Can you find an introduction written by someone other than the author? Why do you think the author sometimes allows someone else to write the introduction?

The Main Text

If you are trying to choose a book in the library, you will not usually have time to read much of the main text to help you to decide which book to choose.

To get the gist of the story you can skim through the book paying particular attention only to the first sentence, chapter headings, illustrations and last paragraph.

Once you decide which book to take away for closer reading, you may read much more slowly and carefully, guessing what comes next and taking time to enjoy it. If it is an information book you may wish to read it slowly and very carefully, paying attention to many details.

Appendix

Sometimes, especially in the case of fiction, the book ends when you get to the last page of the story. But other books have items which come after the main part of the book.

At the end of a book we may find an appendix, or reference section. In this section we may find more information on the subject about which we have been reading. This might be:

1. other books to read on the subject
2. places to visit if you are interested in finding out first hand
3. things you might do if you wish to become more expert in your subject
4. names of people to contact.

Glossary

In the appendix we sometimes find a glossary. This is a list of difficult or unusual words used in the book. It is very helpful to have such a glossary in the appendix as it saves us having to take time to find the words in our dictionaries.

Example
Below are nine words taken from a glossary in an appendix of a book.

steel	—	*prison*
rookeries	—	*slum areas*
esclop	—	*policeman*
shoful	—	*counterfeit money*
rampsman	—	*mugger*
gonoph	—	*petty thief*
fogle	—	*silk handkerchief*
cracksman	—	*safebreaker*
smasher	—	*a passer of counterfeit money*

A 1. The words should be in alphabetical order as in a dictionary. Write them out (with their meanings) in the correct order.
   2. What do you think the book is about?

Index

Most information books have an index, which is very useful for finding the parts of the book you need to look up.

In your own book, write out an answer column numbered 1–10. Refer to the index on the opposite page. Scan very quickly. Write out the number of the page on which you can read about each item mentioned below. Number 1 is done for you. Check that it is correct.

A

You can read about:	on page:
1. DC–8	28, 30, 36

2. hydrogen
3. Trident
4. Wright Brothers
5. Narita Airport
6. Bleriot, Louis

7. helipads
8. sound barrier
9. Ulm, Charles
10. stacking

B
1. Boeing 727
2. gliders
3. navigation
4. flying-boats
5. automatic pilot

6. Vickers Vimy biplane
7. airbus
8. Hindenburg
9. dirigibles
10. R101

C When you require information about a topic which is expressed in a few words, you must decide which is the most important word (or key word). Note it down and look it up. For example, in number 1 the key word is *Concorde*, so we write *1. Concorde*.
Write out the others in the same way.

1. speed of Concorde
2. use of the automatic pilot
3. security on planes
4. find the way by dead reckoning
5. courses in navigation

6. learning to fly gliders
7. career of Amy Johnson
8. the making of helicopters
9. breaking of the sound barrier
10. travel by flying-boat

Now scan through the index and see if it contains each of the words you chose. If you cannot find the word you chose, choose another important word and try the index again.

INDEX

Assignment

Select an information book which contains a glossary and an index. Find at least three terms in the glossary that you don't know much about. See how well you can understand the definitions in the glossary. Then use the index to find a main section of the book dealing with one of your chosen terms. Read more about it in the main part of the book.

Finally write your own helpful definition of the term and see if your friends can understand it. Be prepared to answer their questions.

2. Sources of Information

Magazines

Magazines are a very popular source of reading material. Covers are usually designed in an attractive way to catch the eye of the would-be reader.
A fair amount of information about the magazine is often given on the cover and on the contents page so that our interest can be aroused immediately and we can check quickly and easily whether it contains the type of articles we might wish to read.

HOMES and gardens

No 1708170

GOOD MORNING AMERICA
Fabulous houses/Furnishings/Fashion

Delicious homemade sweets
The new look for glamorous kitchens
Why modern men need
a shoulder to cry on

CONTENTS

November 1981
Number 5 Volume 63

Homes and Gardens
Incorporating "Home"
King's Reach Tower,
Stamford Street,
London SE1 9LS

Cover: *graphic designer, Sewell Sillman's eighteenth-century farmhouse in Connecticut. Photograph by Michael Dunne.*

Editor
Jenny Greene 261 5678

Personal Assistant
Frances Iley 261 5678

Deputy Editor
Primrose Minney 261 6108

Assistant Editor/Art Editor
Joy Hanington 261 5826

Deputy Art Editor
Michael Lyons 261 5686

Assisted by
Elizabeth Galbraith 261 5686

Chief Sub-editor
Jane Taylor 261 6056

Deputy Chief Sub-editor
Chris Howe 261 6074

Sub-editors
Nicola Mitchell 261 6028
Claire Foot 261 6038

Features Editor
Paddy Burt 261 6181

Home Interests Editor
Freda Parker 261 6222

Home Interests Deputy Editor
Rosalind Burdett 261 6325

Assisted by
Christopher Sheldon 261 6260
Helen Barnett 261 6347

Fashion and Beauty Editor
Jean Scroggie 261 5439

Assisted by
Lucilla Deane 261 6202

Special Projects Editor
Christine Coleman 261 6373

Staff Photographer
John Miller 261 6098

Advertisement Manager
John Burnett 261 5072

General Enquiries *261 6099*

A 1. What is the magazine on page 16 called?
   2. How often is it published? How do you know?
   3. Study the last five lines on the cover.
       What is the meaning of (a) fabulous
                              (b) delicious
                              (c) glamorous?
   4. Why do you think those words are used on the cover?
   5. What is the main difference between the arrangement of the contents on page 17 and the contents page of the book on page 7?
   6. What would be the advantages of the arrangement in this magazine contents page?
   7. Who is the editor?
   8. What is the telephone number for enquiries?
   9. Note that there is an index to advertisers. Why do you think advertisers advertise in magazines?
   10. Why would magazine editors encourage advertisements in their magazines?

B 1. What is the magazine shown opposite called?
   2. What do you think might be an advantage of putting the contents list on the cover instead of inside?
   3. Can you give some possible reasons for showing five items from the contents list in large letters down the left-hand side of the page? (eg. "How the weather changes you" is in the contents list and set out in bold letters on the left as well.)
   4. What other information is there on the cover that might encourage people to read the magazine regularly?
   5. Why do you think "£100 for Your Letter" is mentioned on the cover page? Why might the editor have decided on page 1 for this item?

Assignment

Go to your library and study two magazines. For each magazine note down (if you can find the information):
1. the name of the magazine;
2. how often it is published;
3. where it is published;
4. whether it has a contents page;
5. whether it has an index;
6. who the editor is;
7. the address to which you could write to order the magazine;
8. how the cover is made to appear attractive.

Reader's Digest

April 1982

85p

How the Weather Changes You
PAGE 78

FALSE PROMISE OF NUCLEAR PEACE
PAGE 39

NEWMARKET, Home of Racing

ALEC McCOWEN'S GOSPEL HIT
PAGE 126

Flying With the Red Arrows
PAGE 60

=== **Book Choice** ===

The Children Who Didn't Belong
by TOREY HAYDEN
A young teacher shares the heart-stopping tragedies
and triumphs of her 'disturbed' pupils
PAGE 157

£100 for Your Letter, 1; It Pays to Enrich Your
Word Power, 9; All to the Good, 23;
Points to Ponder, 35

World's most read magazine
31 million copies – 41 editions– 17 languages

Brochure

You are now going to practise finding information quickly. First of all, in your own book make an answer column like that started on page 20. Imagine you are considering a holiday in Greece or the Greek Islands, but wish to find out more information before you decide.

19

On the opposite page is a list of information from a holiday brochure which might give you the details you need. Keep in mind the words underlined in each question and glance rapidly down the list until you find them. Write out in your own answer column the number of the page (or pages) you should refer to. See how quickly you can find each one. Number 1 has been done for you.

A   If you wished to find out about:

	Answer Column
1. places to stay in <u>Halkidiki</u>	1. 78–83

2. <u>how to book</u>
3. <u>children's discounts</u>
4. possible <u>cruises</u>
5. <u>flight details</u>
6. cost of <u>insurance</u>
7. cost of <u>car hire</u>
8. the city of <u>Athens</u>
9. resorts in <u>Rhodes</u>
10 Greece's <u>small islands</u>
11. savings on <u>group bookings</u>

B   Many small places are mentioned under the headings Corfu, Crete, Rhodes, Kos and Kalynnos, Halkidiki, Athens, and Small Islands.

For example: Heraklion is under the heading, Crete. We shall find the information somewhere on pages 44–57.

If you wished to find out about:

1. Tolon	1. 90–103

2. Paleocastritsa
3. Roda
4. Corfu Town
5. Stalis
6. Chania
7. Kassandra
8. Paros
9. Lesbos
10. Rhodes Town
11. Dassia

Did you notice that it is more difficult to work rapidly when the words are not in alphabetical order?

Assignment

Use a school atlas and see how many of the places mentioned in this list you can find on the map.

Shopping Guide

A You will find the answers on the page opposite. Keep in mind the word (or words) underlined. Glance rapidly over the list until you find it. Then write down the name of the shop. Number 1 has been done for you.

1. Where might you have your   *Answer column*
    photograph taken?   1. Hendersons

2. Where would you go if you were interested in ladies' fashions?
3. Where could you buy jewellery?
4. In which shop could you buy antique furniture?
5. Which shop will sell television sets?
6. In which restaurant would you expect French food?
7. Where would it be possible to hire a car?
8. Which might be a good shop in which to buy a hat?
9. Where would one go for picture framing?
10. Name a flower shop.

B In this exercise you will have to read very rapidly twice in order to find the answer.
1. Keep the name of the shop in mind. Find it in the list and remember its number.
2. Look for the number on the map and this will tell you the street it is in.
    For example: Deeside Frames is in _____ Street.
    (a) *Deeside Frames.* We look through the list and see its number is 8.
    (b) We look at the map and check that it is in Chapel Street.
    Answer: Deeside Frames is in *Chapel* Street.

Do numbers 1 to 5 in the same way. Work very quickly.
1. Gerard's Restaurant is in _____ Street.
2. West End Florist is in _____ Street.
3. Alexanders is in _____ Street.
4. Nova is in _____ Street.
5. Mitchells Self Drive is in _____ Street.

CHAPEL STREET, ROSE STREET and THISTLE STREET

Chapel, Rose and Thistle are the names of streets forming an interesting shopping area of great character, just off the west end of Union Street.

Within a few steps of each other, the traders in this area offer an extremely wide range of goods to attract the interest of the discerning shopper.

In addition to limited street parking, a multi-storey car park nearby will allow the visitor more time to appreciate the atmosphere of the area.

1.
Colin Wood Antiques Ltd
Antique Furniture and Objets d'Art
Telephone 23019

2.
Hendersons
Photography and Film Specialists
Telephone 24365

3.
Kay Ross & Daughter
Hats for Ladies and Gents
Telephone 28636

4.
West End Florist
Interflora Florists
Telephone 52271/2

5.
Annabel Fashions
Ladies Fashions
Telephone 51989

6.
Mitchells Self Drive
Car and Van Hire
Telephone 50305

7.
Gerards Restaurant
French Restaurant
Telephone 571782

8.
Deeside Frames
Picture Gallery and framing Service
Telephone 28282

7.
Nova
Gifts, Jewellery, Toys, Kitchen Ware
Telephone 21270

10.
Alexanders
Radio, T.V., Audios
Telephone 53319

London Underground Map

At the foot of this page there is a map of part of the London Underground. Beside the name of each station in lists A and B there should be a map reference but they are not complete. (*For example:* Colindale G___. From the information given we see that Colindale is in column G. We look quickly up column G and find Colindale in row 3. The answer is G3.)

A Write out the answers (as in the example above) for each of the following:

1. Hatton Cross A___
2. Hillingdon A___
3. Harrow on the Hill D___
4. East Acton D___
5. Turnham Green C___
6. London Bridge M___
7. St Paul's L___
8. Arsenal M___
9. Woodford O___
10. Bethnal Green N___

B In this exercise we are given the row but not the column. See how quickly you can complete the following:

(*Example:* Turnpike Lane ___3. *Answer:* M3.)

1. Tower Hill ___6
2. Bond Street ___6
3. Cannon Street ___7
4. Chiswick Park ___7
5. Gloucester Road ___7
6. Gunnersbury ___7
7. Hounslow Central ___7
8. Kew Gardens ___8
9. Parson's Green ___8
10. Richmond ___8

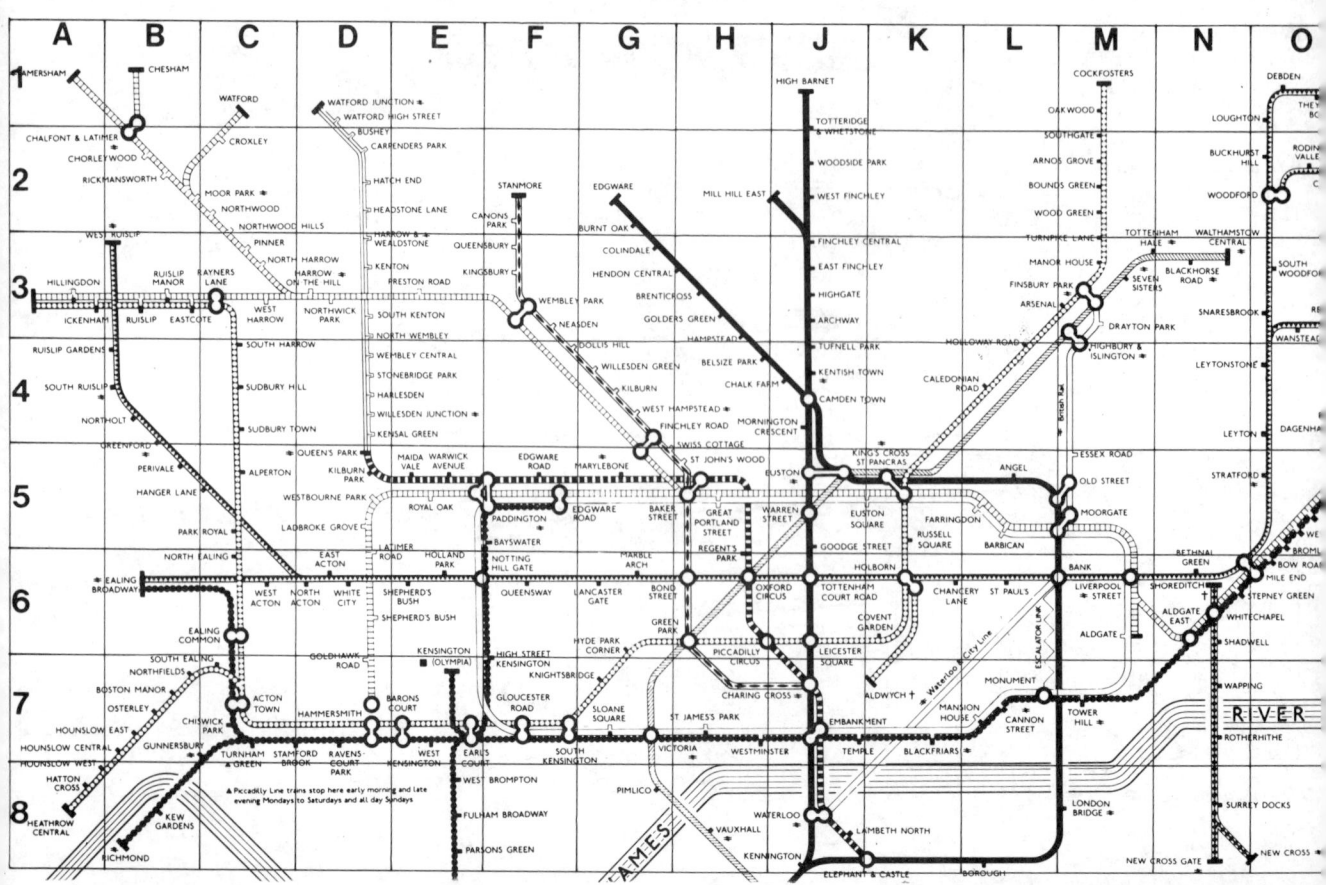

C For 1 to 10 below write down the name of the station at which you think one would need to change trains when making a journey from:

(*Example:* Bank to Aldgate.   *Answer:* Liverpool Street)

1. Whitechapel to Leyton
2. Walthamstow Central to Wood Green
3. Highgate to Brentcross
4. Baker Street to Lancaster Gate
5. South Kensington to Pimlico
6. Green Park to St James' Park
7. Bond Street to Bayswater
8. Chancery Lane to Russell Square
9. Notting Hill Gate to Kilburn Park
10. Waterloo to Mansion House

AA Handbook

The *AA Members' Handbook* contains a great deal of information written out in a very concise form. This is made possible by using a key.

Page 149 of 1982/83 AA Handbook and keys from the inside front cover and page 25 are printed on pages 26, 27 and 28.

Example
Cutty Sark Inn, MARAZION. We are told the address, phone number, number of bedrooms, number of parking places and price of bed and breakfast.

For some of these details you must use the keys.

A According to the information given on the following pages:
1. (a) Which would be the most luxurious hotel listed? What tells you this?
   (b) Is it open all the year round. How can you tell?
   (c) How much would bed and breakfast cost you?
   (d) For how many cars would there be parking spaces?

2. How far is
   (a) Manston from London?
   (b) Market Drayton from London?
   (c) Market Rasen from London?

3. Write out and complete the following:
      Grove Motel is situated in _____ Road, _____.
   The telephone number is _____. It has 25
   rooms with _____. Dogs are _____. There are
   parking places for _____. The charges for bed and
   breakfast are _____ to _____.

MANNINGTREE 358 Essex Map20TM13 *Colchester9*
Harwich11 Ipswich15 *London70*
Bridge Cattawade ☎2755 R22.00
MANSFIELD 58,450 Notts Map25SK56 EcWed
MdThu/Fri/Sat/cattle Mon Chesterfield *London140*
Newark19 *Nottingham14*
 ★★**Midland** Midland Pl ☎24668 27rm(20↩🍴) 18P B&B*(c)*
Chatfield-Martin Walter Nottingham Rd ☎26101
☎26723 🔧 Vau Opl
Bewac Mtrs Southwell Rd West ☎31331 ☎648692
🔧 BL RT
Sherwood Hall Clipstone Rd West, Forest Town
☎27661 ☎23527 🔧
Ladybrook S/Sta Ladybrook Ln ☎25447 ☎640169
Kings Mill (Brian C Hardy) Sutton Rd ☎35411 ☝ Cit
Woods 90 Leeming Ln North, Mansfield Woodhouse
☎23820 ☎640267 ☝
MANSTON Kent Map11TR36 EcThu MdFri Canterbury14
Dover18 London75 Ramsgate3
†**Manston Court** Manston Rd ☎344 ☎Thanet 65009
R20.00
MARAZION 1,475 Cornwall Map4SW53 EcWed Helston10
London292 Penzance3 Redruth17
 ★**Cutty Sark** The Square ☎Penzance 710334 11rm 30P
B&B*(b)*
MARDEN 2,606 Kent Map11TQ74 EcWed Hastings27
London45 Maidstone8 Tunbridge Wells15
Collier Street Collier St ☎Collier Street 321 ☝24hrs 🔧 BL
MARGARETTING 949 Essex Map19TL60 EcWed
Brentwood7 Chelmsford41 *London33*
Speedwell S/Sta Roman Rd ☎Ingatestone 3261
☎Ingatestone 2232 🔧
E Weaver & Sons Myrtle Villa, Main Rd ☎Ingatestone 3224
☝
MARGATE 50,290 Kent Map11TR37 EcThu MdThu/Fri
Canterbury16 *Dover25 London76*
 ★★**Walpole Bay** Fifth Av, Cliftonville (1m E) BW ☎Thanet
21703 C 48rm(18↩) B&B*(b)*
 ★☆**Ye Olde Charles Inn** Northdown Rd, Cliftonville (1m E)
☎Thanet 21817 10rm 20P B&B*(b)(c)*
Palm Bay Northdown Rd ☎Thanet 20919 ☝ 🔧 Ren
Invicta Mtrs Northdown Rd, Cliftonville (1m E) ☎Thanet
26554 🔧 Frd
MARKET BOSWORTH 1,253 Leics Map27SK40
Birmingham37 Hinckley7 Leicester12 *London102*
Station Station Rd ☎290676 ☝ 🔧
MARKET DRAYTON 7,088 Salop Map23SJ63 EcThu MdWed
gen & cattle *London158* Shrewsbury19 Stafford19
Stoke-on-Trent17
 ★★**Corbet Arms** High St ☎2037 9↩ 50P B&B*(c)(d)*
 ★★**Tern Hill** (on A53) ☎Tern Hill 310 11rm(7↩) 🔥 126P
B&B*(c)*
Arnolds Auto Sales and Service Shrewsbury Rd ☎4388 ☝
🔧 Tal Vau Sko
MARKET HARBOROUGH 15,230 Leics Map25SP78 EcWed
MdSat/cattle Tue Kettering11 *London83 Northampton18*
 ★★**Angel** High St ☎63123 18rm 44P B&B*(b)(c)*
 ★★**Grove Motel** Northampton Rd ☎64082 30rm(25↩) 🔥 65P
B&B*(c)(d)*
 ★★**Three Swans** High St ☎66644 18rm(11↩🍴) 72P B&B*(c)*
Regent Autocar Co Leicester Rd ☎67664 ☎Kibworth
2245 ☝24hrs 🔧 BL
Badger Bros Mtr Eng 109 Main St, Lubenham ☎66984 ☝ 🔧
MARKET RASEN 2,520 Lincs Map25TF18 EcThu
MdTue/cattle Wed Grimsby21 *Lincoln16 London158* Louth15
Scunthorpe26
 ★★**Limes** Gainsborough Rd ☎842357 13rm(10↩🍴) 50P
B&B*(c)*
 ★**Gordon Arms** Queen St ☎842364 7rm 🔥 43P
MARKET WEIGHTON 2,584 Humberside Map35SE84 EcThu
Beverley10 Hull18 *London201* York19
 ★★**Ladbroke Londesborough Arms** LB ☎2219 10rm 🔥
100P B&B*(b)(c)*
Armstrong Massey High St ☎2361 ☝ 🔧 BL RT LR
MARKFIELD 3,164 Leics Map25SK40 EcWed Leicester7
London105 Loughborough9 *Nottingham26*
Flying Horse 5/7 Shaw Ln ☎2369 ☎3618
Browns Blue 32 Shaw Ln ☎2171 🔧 Tal
MARKS TEY 1,407 Essex Map20TL92 Braintree10
Chelmsford18 *Colchester6 London55*

☆☆☆**Marks Tey** London Rd ☎Colchester 210001 106↩ 160P
B&B*(c)(d)*
MARKYATE 2,609 Herts Map18TL01 *London30* Dunstable5
Luton4
 ☆☆☆**Hertfordshire Moat House** London Rd (A5) QM
☎Luton 840840 97↩ 200P B&B*(c)(d)*
MARLBOROUGH 6,370 Wilts Map8SU16 EcWed MdWed/Sat
Chippenham19 *London78* Newbury19 Swindon12
 ★★**Ailesbury Arms** High St INT ☎53451 30rm(8↩🍴) 🔥 24P
 ★★**Castle & Ball** High St THF ☎52002 30rm(8↩) 50P B&B*(d)*
Bridge (Dick Lovett Specialist Cars) London Rd ☎52381 🔧
Por
MARLOW 11,940 Bucks Map18SU88 EcWed Henley-on-
Thames8 High Wycombe4 *London35* Maidenhead6
 ★★★★**Compleat Angler** Marlow Br THF ☎4444 42↩ 104P
L B&B*(f)*
Platts (R J E Platt) West St, Oxford Rd ☎2215 ☝ 🔧 BL
Marlow Mtrs 50 Marlow Bottom ☎3112 🔧
MARNHULL 1,627 Dorset Map8ST71 EcWed/Sat Blandford12
Dorchester24 London104 Shaftesbury8
Guys Auto Eng ☎820244 ☎820674 🔧 Maz Lad
MARSH GIBBON 724 Bucks Map18SP62 EcWed/Thu
London56 Aylesbury15 Bicester6 *Oxford19*
Bicester Rd S/Sta Bicester Rd ☎Stratton Audley 304 ☝ ☝
🔧 Rel
MARSHWOOD 303 Dorset Map7SY39 *London144* Bridport8
Lyme Regis8 Yeovil17
Marshwood ☎Hawkchurch 343 ☝20.00 🔧
MARSTON MAGNA 393 Somerset Map7ST52 *London122
Taunton28* Wincanton11 Yeovil5
Marston (Olds) ☎850856 Cit
MARSTON TRUSSELL 188 Northants Map25SP68 *London85*
Market Harborough4 *Northampton19* Rugby16
 ★★**Sun Inn** ☎Market Harborough 65531 10rm(9↩) 🔥 43P
B&B*(c)(d)*
MARTHAM 1,570 Norfolk Map29TG41 EcWed Cromer26
London133 Norwich18 Yarmouth10
Martham Mtrs 2 Rollesby Rd ☎Gt Yarmouth 740247 🔧
MARTINHOE 120 Devon Map6SS64 *Barnstaple18*
Ilfracombe17 *London207* Lynten5 Simonsbath14
 ★♨**Old Rectory** ☎Parracombe 368 C 11rm(6↩🍴) 14P nc6
B&B*(b)(c)*
MARTOCK 2,703 Somerset Map7ST41 Ilchester5 *London129
Taunton21* Yeovil7
 ★**White Hart** ☎822246 10rm 18P B&B*(b)*
Yandles North St ☎822504 🔧 Frd
Bridge (Brooks & Son) Water St ☎822547 ☎822392
☝24hrs 🔧 BL
MARYPORT 11,560 Cumbria Map38NY03 EcWed MdFri
Carlisle28 Keswick20 *London324* Workington6
 ★**Waverley** Curzon St ☎2115 20rm(1↩9🍴) P B&B*(b)*
Dobies Ellenborough ☎5555 ☎Cockermouth 4050 🔧 Fia
Vau
MASHAM 825 N Yorks Map40SE28 EcThu MdWed/cattle Tue
London228 Middlesbrough39 Ripon9 Thirsk15
 ★★♨**Jervaulx Hall** ☎Bedale 60235 C 8rm(3↩) 20P
B&B*(b)(c)*
 ★★**Kings Head** Market Pl ☎295 14rm
Wensleydale (Todd & Sons) ☎202 ☝ 🔧
MATLOCK 20,300 Derbys Map24SK36 EcThu MdTue/Fri
Buxton20 Chesterfield11 Derby18 *London148 Nottingham26*
 ★★★**New Bath** New Bath Rd (2m S A6) THF ☎3275 56↩
250P B&B*(d)*
 ★★♨**Riber Hall** Riber ☎2795 A8↩🍴 🔥 50P nc10
B B&B*(d)(e)*
 ★**High Tor** Artists Corner, Dale Rd ☎2031 18rm(2↩1🍴) 30P
B&B*(b)*
Bakewell Bodywks 11 Bakewell Rd ☎2131 ☎Bakewell
2765 ☝
Kennings Bakewell Rd ☎3291 ☝ 🔧 BL RT LR
Slaters 50 Smedley St East ☎2101 🔧
Matlock Green Matlock Gr ☎3668 R18.30 ☝24hrs ☝ 🔧
Cliff Tansley ☎3207
MATTINGLEY 577 Hants Map9SU75 EcWed Basingstoke9
London44 Reading11
Hound Green ☎Heckfield 242 R19.30 🔧
MAULDEN 1,959 Beds Map18TL03 EcWed Ampthill1
Bedford8 *London45*

149

Abbreviations and Symbols

For how to read a gazetteer entry see page 90

General entries

▧	AA office (see pages 5–13)	ex	except
☎	telephone ⎤ *unless stated, the*	fy	ferry
	name of the exchange	Map	figures and letters which follow give
☏	night *is the same as the*		the service atlas page number and
	telephone *placename; at hotels*		the national grid reference (see atlas
	the number is usually		page 64)
	for reception only	Md	market day

▧   AA office (see pages 5–13)

☎   telephone ⎤ *unless stated, the
name of the exchange
is the same as the
placename; at hotels
the number is usually
for reception only*

☏   night telephone

D   district (see 'Population', page 90)

Ec   early closing

ex   except

fy   ferry

Map   figures and letters which follow give the service atlas page number and the national grid reference (see atlas page 64)

Md   market day

Note: only those places having AA-appointed establishments are included in the gazetteer

Garage entries

†   details not confirmed

✻   garage classification (see page 19)

🏍   Free Breakdown Service classification; service normally available 24 hours every day, unless otherwise shown (see page 19)

🏍   motorcycle specialist classification (see page 19)

🏍   Free Breakdown Service available Monday–Friday during normal working hours, unless otherwise stated

🏍   motorcycle and/or scooter repairs undertaken

✠   approved vehicle testing station at time of going to press; it is advisable to confirm by telephone

mdnt   service until midnight

R   repairs and servicing available *outside* normal working hours until time shown

Vau *etc*   abbreviations for franchises held by garages (see page 92)

Hotel entries

★   hotel classification (see page 25)

★   hotel classification (see page 25)

☆   hotel classification (see page 25)

⊕   approved hotel (see page 25)

○   hotel likely to open during the currency of the *Handbook*

⬥   country-house hotel (see page 25)

H B L   merit award (see page 25)

❀   rosette award (see page 25)

Ⓖ   mainly grill-type meals

THF *etc*   abbreviations for hotel groups (see page 91)

C   closed for two months or more within a year (see page 91)

CC   closed for less than two months at any one time (see page 91)

RS   restricted services operate for a period (see page 91)

U   unlicensed

rm   number of bedrooms (see page 91)

⇔🚿   private bathroom and/or shower with own toilet (see page 91)

A   annexe (followed by number of rooms)

🐕   no dogs

P   parking on hotel premises (number of cars usually stated)

🅿   no parking available on hotel premises

nc   no children *eg* nc4 = no children under 4 years of age

Hotel charges

The price-banding system used in the *Handbook* indicates the range within which each hotel's lowest charge for bed and breakfast (per single room, including VAT and service charge where applicable) is likely to fall. Double room prices are not always double the single room prices. Note that where a hotel's 1982 prices are already close to the top of a band (or where 1981 prices only have been given) the next band up has also been given.

Published price-bands, based on information provided by hoteliers during summer 1981, must therefore be accepted as indications rather than firm estimates.

Prices should always be checked before booking as they are likely to change during the currency of the *Handbook* – affected by inflation, possible variations in the rate of VAT and indeed many other factors.

Price-band	Charges	Price-band	Charges
a	up to £10	*d*	£20 to £30
b	£10 to £15	*e*	£30 to £40
c	£15 to £20	*f*	over £40

Hotels

The star classification of hotels by the AA, in addition to providing an indication of the type of hotel, may be regarded as a universally accepted standard in all classifications, from the simplest inn to the most luxurious hotel. It should be remembered that some hotels may satisfy several of the requirements of a classification higher than that awarded.

The majority of hotels are indicated by black stars, the method introduced and used by the AA since 1912 to indicate hotels offering traditional hospitality and service in traditional accommodation.

★ Hotels and inns generally of small scale with acceptable facilities and furnishings. All bedrooms with hot and cold water; adequate bath and lavatory arrangements. Meals are provided for residents but their availability to non-residents may be limited.

★★ Hotels offering a higher standard of accommodation and some private bathrooms/showers. A wider choice of food is provided but the availabiity of meals to non-residents may be limited.

★★★ Well-appointed hotels with more spacious accommodation with a large number of bedrooms with private bathrooms/showers. Fuller meal facilities are provided but for luncheon and at weekends service to non-residents may be restricted.

★★★★ Exceptionally well-appointed hotels offering a high standard of comfort and service with the majority of bedrooms providing private bathrooms/showers.

★★★★★ Luxury hotels offering the highest international standards.

⊕ Hotels which conform to most star classification requirements and are worthy of recommendation.

♠ The symbol used to denote an AA Country House hotel where a relaxed informal atmosphere and personal welcome prevail. However, some of the facilities may differ from those found in urban hotels of the same classification.

These hotels are often secluded but not always rurally situated.

White stars

☆ The method used to indicate establishments high in amenities but with deliberately limited personalised services designed and operated to cater predominantly for the short-stay guest. Under this heading will be found some motels and motor hotels with bedroom facilities mainly on a self-service basis. It is emphasised that white stars are an indication of a type of hotel.

Assignment

Look up a town in your area in the AA Handbook. Choose a hotel that you would recommend to someone who has to stay overnight on business. Make up your own mind how they will be travelling (eg. car, train, plane). Give some of your reasons for your choice of hotel. (Remember that, although business travellers do not usually have to pay the bill out of their own pocket, their employers might not be too happy with the most expensive place you can find!)

A   1. Why do you think a play on TV about an accident at work (9.08 am) might be more effective than articles in newspapers or magazines?

MONDAY tv

BBC 1

9.8 am
For Schools, Colleges
9.8 Going to Work
Health and Safety
A play for discussion by JOHN TULLY
Alan Fiske lies unconscious in hospital – another victim of an accident at work. But what happened? Who was to blame?
with JOHN ALTMAN, DAVID PUGH, SYD GOLDER, FRANK TAYLOR, ERIC MASON, MARGARET STALLARD, RICHARD GRAY
Producer GEOFF WILSON

9.33 A Good Job with Prospects
Specialist Civil Servants
Civil servants help people working on land, at sea and in the air.
Narrator JOHN DUNN
Producer JILL SHEPPARD

10.0 You and Me
Stretch and Run (Repeat)

10.15
For Schools, Colleges
10.15 Music Time
Collecting Sounds: 7 (Repeat)
10.38 British Social History
Man Made the Slave by ALAN PLATER
The story of Thomas Cooper and the Leicester Chartists
with DAVID NEAL, MARTIN FRIEND
DONALD MCKILLOP, JOHN ROWE
JAMES GREENE, RICHARD KAYE
PAUL RIDLEY, JOSEPH LONG
Concertina JOHN NIXON
Consultant PETER SEARBY
Produced by RONALD SMEDLEY
11.0 Let's See. *Your Health*
A three-programme unit which considers some basic concepts of health education. 3: Breakdown
Two children become hospital patients for the first time. One is an out-patient, taken to Casualty with a broken leg after a road accident. The other is going in for a longer stay in order to have an operation.
Director PETER LEGGE
Series producer MARIANNE BAIRD
11.23 Talkabout
Two of Everything (Repeat)
11.42 General Studies. *The Biggest Epidemic of our Times: 2*
Motorcycles are the greatest killers of young people in peacetime Britain.
(First shown in Man Alive on BBC2)
12.7 pm Closedown

12.30 News After Noon
Richard Whitmore and Moira Stuart

12.55
The Scottish News

1.0 Pebble Mill at One
Including: *Langley South*

1.45 Chock-a-Block
A *See-Saw* programme *(Repeat)*

2.1
For Schools, Colleges
2.1 Words and Pictures
Wicked Wolf (Repeat)
2.18 Read On!
In Your Own Time (Repeat)
2.40 Out of the Past
Georgian England (Repeat)

3.0 See Hear!
(Shown yesterday at 12.10 pm)

3.25 Delia Smith's
Cookery Course
A series of ten programmes
6: *Sauces (Repeat)*
Delia Smith recipe on Ceefax page **167**

3.53 Regional News (exc London)

3.55 Play School
Story: *A Great Day for Up*
Written by DR SEUSS
Pictures by QUENTIN BLAKE
Presenters
Sheelagh Gilbey, Don Spencer
(Shown on BBC2 at 11.0 am)

4.20* The Return
of the Space Shuttle
A *Newsround* special
After five days orbiting the Earth, America's space shuttle *Columbia* re-enters the atmosphere to touch down at Edwards Air Force Base, California. Live coverage introduced by **John Craven** in London, and reports from **Reg Turnill** at Mission Control in Houston.
Studio director PETER DAVIDSON
Producer LEWIS BRONZE
Executive producer ERIC ROWAN

4.40 Jigsaw
A picture puzzle series starring **Adrian Hedley, Janet Ellis** and **Tommy Boyd** with **Sylvester McCoy** and **David Rappaport** as the O-Men
Onager is the name of an ass. Watch out for double D words and the land of Peatopia. The giggling monster Di Larfing interrupts with some awful jokes. The competition jigword is more difficult than last week. If you can't understand any of this it doesn't matter.

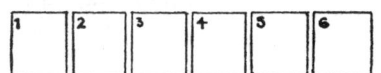

Graphics ANDY COWARD
Director RICHARD SIMKIN
Written and produced by CLIVE DOIG

5.5 Newsround
with **Paul McDowell**

5.10-5.40
Blue Peter
with **Simon Groom, Sarah Greene** and **Peter Duncan**

2. Which words in the *Radio Times* suggest there may not be one simple explanation for this accident?
3. What would you expect to be shown on the 9.33 programme? Who would be particularly interested in it?
4. Where might you get information about the 10 o'clock programme?
5. What is an epidemic (11.42)?
6. How much time is given over to news programmes in this part of the day? Which one might be most liable to cancellation? Why?
7. What might be the advantages of showing a cookery programme on television?
8. Why is there a note in brackets on some occasions that a programme is a repeat? Why do you think there are so many repeats in programmes for schools and colleges?
9. In "Jigsaw" why do you think there is a sentence at the end to say that it does not matter if you have not understood the paragraph?
10. To which part of the UK do these programmes apply? How do you know?

Assignments

1. *For each channel (BBC1, BBC2, ITV) find out how much time was given over last week to (a) entertainment (b) schools and colleges (including Open University) (c) documentaries (d) news programmes. Represent the information in graph form and compare the balance in each.*
2. *Make a note of the programmes you watch during one week. Compare your list with others in your class.*

Recipe

Chocolate-coated Coconut Ice

Ingredients

Cochineal, $\frac{1}{4}$ pint milk, 150 g. plain chocolate (melted), 500 g. desiccated coconut, 1 kilo granulated sugar, 1 teaspoon vanilla essence, $\frac{1}{4}$ pint water.

Put the milk, $\frac{1}{4}$ pint water and the sugar into a solid-based pan. Stir over a gentle heat until the sugar has dissolved. Bring to the boil and boil to 115°C, 238–240°F. Remove the pan from the heat, add the coconut and vanilla essence, and beat until the mixture reaches a consistency that is thick and creamy.

Pour half the mixture into a greased shallow 8in. sq. tin. Quickly colour the remaining mixture with cochineal and pour over the white layer. Leave in a cool place to set.

Cut through into 1 in. strips and carefully remove from the tin in complete strips. Stand them on a wire rack and coat evenly with melted chocolate. Leave until set.

Using a very sharp knife cut into small pieces. Put into paper cases and pack in boxes.

A 1. Write out the ingredients in the order you will require them. (One on each line.)
$\frac{1}{4}$ pint milk
$\frac{1}{4}$ pint water, etc.
2. List in order the utensils you will require:
solid-based pan, etc.
3. Make a flow diagram to show the steps in making chocolate-coated coconut ice.

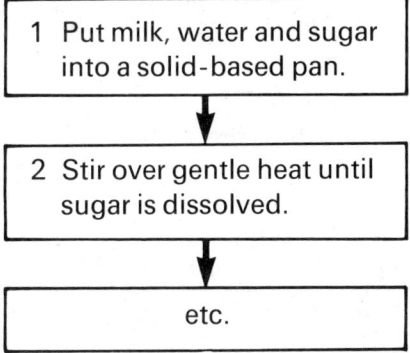

Yellow Pages

Opposite is part of a page from a *Yellow Pages Telephone Directory*. From this you can find out a great deal of information.

A What is the telephone number of the following?
1. Civic Sports
2. John R Carstairs
3. Champion Sports
4. I G Meiklejohn and Co. Ltd.
5. A C Sportswear

B If you wished to buy sportswear or other sports goods you would normally go to a Sports Goods Shop and not a wholesaler.
To which of the following would you go?
1. Elliott Sports Co.
2. Blues Sport
3. Ben Sayers Ltd.
4. Dunlop Sports Co.
5. Kugar Golf Ltd.

C At which shop might you buy equipment for these sports?
1. tennis   2. fencing   3. darts   4. keep-fit

To which shop might you go for advice on the following?
5. engraving of trophies   6. golf club repairs

To which shop might you go for some item of sportsgear not mentioned by name on the page opposite (eg. running shoes)? Why?

D Where would you go if you wished to find information about:
1. skates
2. tents and other items for camping
3. Elliott Sports Company and Ronnie Simpson Sports will have to pay extra for large advertisements on the yellow page. Why might they find it worth doing so?
4. What advantage can you see in having a separate yellow pages directory with, for example, all sports shops in the same section?

Assignment

Consult your local yellow pages directory. Write down the name, address and telephone number of one of each of the following types of shop which you know how to reach.
> *Pet shop*
> *Cafe*
> *Supermarket*
> *TV supplier*
> *Hairdresser*

◆ Sound Equipment Installation Contractors

ASTRAL SOUND—
Sound System Instl/Mfrs For All Comm. Premises,
Pontyberem,Dyfed.................................**Pontyberem** 249
CALEDONIAN TELEPHONE Co.Ltd,
11 Randolph Pl,Edinburgh 3 ....031–225 3553

◆ Spinners

SEE ALSO FLAX AND HEMP MANUFACTURERS AND
SPINNERS: YARN SPINNERS

Clough Mill Ltd, Waverley Mill...................**Innerleithen** 830531
(Telex 72665)
Ettrick & Yarrow Spinners Ltd, Ettrick Mill..........**Selkirk** 20782
(Telex 72577)
Hall A.& Sons Ltd, Langlands Mill,Newtown.....**St. Boswells** 2244
Hallwool—
Langlands Mill,Newtown St. Boswells ....**St. Boswells** 2323
Laidlaw & Fairgrieve Ltd—
Ladhope Mills..**Galashiels** 3286
(Telex 72193)
Stewarts Spinners (Galashiels) Ltd,
Waukrigg Mill...**Galashiels** 3277
Weensland Spinning Co.Ltd—
Weensland Mill..**Hawick** 2509
(Telex 727845)
Wright & Jobson Ltd, Bristol Mill.....................**Galashiels** 2560

◆ Sports Centres

SEE LEISURE CENTRES

◆ Sports Clubs

SEE CLUBS AND ASSOCIATIONS—SPORTS

◆ Sports Equipment Manufacturers and Wholesalers

SEE ALSO NET MANUFACTURERS

Adventure Equipment (Wholesale) Ltd,
172 Easter Rd 7...031–661 1318
Carstairs John R, The Links.............................**Leven** 26381
Daiwa Golf (Scotland) Ltd, Tantallon Rd ....**N Berwick** 3831
Dunbar Golf Co.(Scotland) Ltd,
East Barns School...**Dunbar** 63060
Dunlop Sports CO Ltd, 12 Gayfield Sq 1 ....031–556 0040
Edinburgh Golf & Sports Co.Ltd, Clockmill ....**Duns** 3216
Field Sports Scotland, 5 Bruce St.................**Dunfermline** 22435
Homesport Ltd, 12 Whitehill Rd ....**Glenrothes** 771969

KUGARGOLF Ltd—
Custom Made Golf Clubs & Repairs Matched Sets.,
Kingston ....**N Berwick** 3500
Ledgard Chris Golf Gloves Ltd,
Mayfield Cott,Loch Rd...**Saline** 751
Mackay George, Flat 7,65 Blackfriars St 1............031–556 1779
Meiklejohn I.G.& Co,Ltd,
Kingslaw Wks,Junction Rd...**Kirkcaldy** 51054
Nicoll George of Scotland Ltd, Golf Wks................**Leven** 23924
St. Andrew Golf Co.Ltd, 48 Headwell Rd ....**Dunfermline** 36615
Sayers Ben Ltd, 1 Tantallon Rd.......................**N Berwick** 2219
(Telex 727870)
Scot Kites, 225 Granton Rd 5.:.......................031–551 1075
Sports Conscious Screenprint, 1 Brougham Pl 3......031–229 7647
Symca (Edinburgh) Ltd, 2/10 Jeffrey St 1............031–556 2704
Symca (Edinburgh) Ltd, 2/10 Jeffrey St 1............031–556 5939

◆ Sports Goods Shops

SEE ALSO CAMPING EQUIPMENT SUPPLIERS

A.C.Sportswear, 55 Ratcliffe Ter 9......................031–668 2532
Blues Sport, 1 Wemyss Pl 2..............................031–225 9240
Border Archery Ltd, Mellerstains Estates...............**Gordon** 295
Champion Sports, 3 Dalry Rd 11 ....031–229 1563
Civic Sports, 4 Civic Centre.........................**Tranent** 610892
Coughtrie Stan (Sports) Ltd,
18 Almondvale Sth,Regional Centre...**Livingston** 34822
D'Main Sport Shop,
19 Main St,Davidson's Mains,4...031–336 7007

Kean Sport, 87 High St,Dalkeith.......................031–663 1859
Leisure Time Sports Shop, 52 Market St..........**Haddington** 2757
LEISUREWISE,
35 Channel St ....**Galashiels** 56166

Leith Athletics Ltd, 1 Meadowbank Ave 8.............031–661 7664
Lillywhites, 129 Princes St 2 ....031–225 5831
(Telex 727354)
Lillywhites International,
Murrayfield Ice Rink,Murrayfield 12...031–337 2143
LIVINGSTON SPORTS—
A Stan Coughtrie (Sports) LTD Shop,
18 Almondvale S...................................**Livingston** 34822
Luke Ian, 28 Howe St 3 ....031–226 2942
McDonald D & H, 9/11 High St ....**Selkirk** 21398
Mackenzie's Sports Shops Ltd—
17 Nicolson St 8 ....031–667 2288
MacSports, 13 Market St ....**Coldstream** 2868
Mealyou T.H—
(Sports Outftr), 11 Newbiggin,Musselburgh 031–665 2671
Murray J.E, Baberton Golf Club,Juniper Gn...........031–441 1255
Penicuik Sports Co Ltd, 5b West St.....................**Penicuik** 76842
Rankin Tom, 4 Ochilview Sq............................**Armadale** 30449
Robertson J.& Son, 17 North St. Andrew St 2 ......031–556 6332

Scotia Sporting Enterprises, 38 Merchiston Av 10...031–229 7812
Simpson Ronnie, 200 Rose St 2.........................031–225 3857

SECTION B
What Does It Mean?

3. Dictionary

Alphabetical Order

It is important that you should master alphabetical order if you are going to use a dictionary expertly.

A   Write out the words in A, in B, and in C in alphabetical order. (In A pay particular attention to the **third** letter in each word.)

beige	begin	bemoan	betray
beaver	befit	beneath	bevel
bedraggle	behind	beseech	beyond
becalm	belch	beret	bewitch
beech	bejewel	bequeath	bezel

B   (Pay particular attention to the **fourth** letter in each word.)

sail	sallow	same	satin	scalp
saint	salmon	sand	saucer	scant
saki	salt	sanity	saunter	scamp
sake	saloon	sane	savour	scary
sale	salute	sark	save	scape
salad	salver	sarong	scabbard	scatter
salient	sampan	Saturday	scaffold	scaup

34

C

galliard	gambol	garlic	garrulous
gallant	gambit	garland	garrison
gallery	ganglion	garret	gasometer
gallop	gangway	garnish	gasoline
gamble	gangrene	garrotte	genie
			genial
			genius

Check in your dictionary that you have got the words in the correct order in each section.

Definitions

You often use the dictionary to find the definition (the exact meaning) of a word. Many words have more than one definition. You must choose the correct definition to suit the sentence.

A Number 1–11 in your book and write out the word underlined in each sentence. Beside it write the definition from your dictionary which best suits the sentence. Number 1 is done for you.

1. The old salt had travelled several times round the world. (*Answer* salt – a sailor)
2. In the old days people often used salt to preserve the meat.
3. Tom did not grasp what the teacher was talking about.
4. Mary attempted to grasp her brother as he fell into the pool.
5. The driver decided to travel slowly as the line might be blocked with snow.
6. For the Queen's visit all the ships sailed in line.
7. The outlaw was taken by force to the station.
8. All off-duty members of the force were called in to assist with the search.
9. The people faced starvation because of the shortage of grain.
10. Margaret was careful not to spill one grain of sugar.
11. The joiner told the apprentice not to plane the wood against the grain.

B Number 1–10 in your book. Write out the word underlined in each sentence and the definition in your dictionary which best suits the sentence.

1. Elaine was <u>playing</u> Portia in the school's production of "The Merchant of Venice".
2. Yvonne was <u>playing</u> the piano all evening.
3. The gallery was held up by hexagonal <u>columns</u>.
4. The <u>columns</u> of troops stretched for miles further than the spectators could see.
5. The police <u>directed</u> the traffic along an entirely new diversion.
6. Graham did exactly as he had been <u>directed</u> by his father.
7. The captain had been on duty for three <u>watches</u> without a break.
8. Bob carried two <u>watches</u>, a pocket one and a wrist one.
9. Arnold was dragging the sledge when he <u>slumped</u> in the snow.
10. The value of the pound <u>slumped</u> alarmingly when David was abroad on holiday.

Did you find the words *playing*, *columns*, *directed*, *watches* and *slumped*? Some dictionaries do not give words formed by adding endings such as *s*. No doubt you looked up *play*, *column*, *direct*, *watch* and *slump* as it is from these words that the words in the sentences are formed.

C Some words have many meanings.
Write out the meaning of each word underlined. Use your dictionary to help you.

1. James was ordered to get up and <u>wash</u> before breakfast.
2. It looked as if the river would <u>wash</u> away the rest of the embankment.
3. Mother always did the weekly <u>wash</u> on Mondays.
4. The art teacher told the pupil that a blue <u>wash</u> was all that was needed for a background in the painting.
5. The small boat rocked and rolled in the <u>wash</u> of the liner.

D 1. Paul's father said he would <u>make</u> him do his homework.
2. Sheila tried to <u>make</u> the model out of cardboard.
3. Angela did not <u>make</u> it in time to catch the train.
4. The members of the committee wanted to <u>make</u> Mr Smith their chairman.
5. The people at the back of the hall could not <u>make</u> out what the speaker was saying.
6. The watch was of a foreign <u>make</u>.

E
1. The <u>point</u> of his pencil kept breaking; the lead was very brittle.
2. In decimal fractions it is important to put the <u>point</u> in the correct place.
3. The speaker missed the <u>point</u> of the question he was asked.
4. James and Anne had reached the <u>point</u> of disagreement.
5. The judges knew what <u>points</u> to look for when they judged the animals at the show.
6. The trains crashed because the <u>points</u> were frozen.
7. The helmsman was ordered to change course three <u>points</u> to starboard.
8. The judge tried to <u>point</u> out to the prisoner the error of his ways.
9. Every gun was <u>pointed</u> at the enemy.
10. After the frost had damaged the mortar the builder had to <u>point</u> the wall.

Suffixes

If a dictionary does not list a word with a common ending or a suffix, look up the word from which it is derived.

A From which words are the following derived? Number 1 is done for you.
1. airiness (*Answer* air)
2. bilious
3. coverlet
4. falsify
5. familiar
6. girlish
7. looker-on
8. materialism
9. mindless
10. modification
11. provocation
12. reducible
13. scientific
14. sniffler
15. watery

B Number 1–10 in your book. Write out the word underlined and use your dictionary to work out the definition that suits the sentence. Number 1 is done for you.

1. The factory was warned against <u>dumping</u> waste in the quarry.
   (*Answer* dumping – tipping)

2. David had not <u>accomplished</u> much after two days of hard work.
3. There were three <u>applicants</u> for one job.
4. The boys kept <u>battling</u> their way to the summit.

37

5. The inhabitants of the island were very <u>clannish</u> and did not welcome newcomers.
6. The peace negotiations had to be handled with <u>delicacy</u>.
7. All the employees hoped for an <u>enhancement</u> in salary.
8. The doctor feared that the patient might be suffering from a <u>malignant</u> disease.
9. In the shallow water the Captain ordered <u>soundings</u> to be taken every two minutes.
10. The instructor's explanation was not very clear. Mark was seeking some further <u>illumination</u>.

Abbreviations

Many dictionaries help you to decide on the correct definition to choose by the use of abbreviations.

v., v.i., or v.t. all mean *verb*; n. means *noun*; adj. means *adjective*; adv. means *adverb*.

Example
silver *n.*, soft white metal; *adj.* made of silver, bright; *v.t.* to coat with silver.
   After **silver** we see the letter *n*. This means the definition which follows will define silver as a noun.
   When we see the word *silver* in a sentence it will help us if we can decide whether silver is a *noun*, or an *adjective* or a *verb* in the sentence.
   If it is a noun we shall look at the definition which follows *n*. For example, silver is mined in Peru. Silver is a *Noun*. We select the definition which follows *n*.
   James had silver coins in his pocket. Silver is an *adjective*. We would select a definition which follows *adj*.

A   Number 1–12. Write out each word underlined. After each word write *n.*, *adj.*, or *v*. Select the definition in your dictionary which best suits the sentence.

   Example
   The guide explained that the <u>buttress</u> belonged to the oldest part of the building.

      buttress *n.* projecting support of a wall.

   1. After his holiday he felt a <u>moderate</u> improvement in his health.
   2. The yachtsman hoped the strong wind would <u>moderate</u>.

3. Flooding of the playing fields in winter was a perennial problem.
4. The only flowers Mr. Lam had in his garden were perennials.
5. The nurse put a compress on the wound.
6. The baker compressed the dough into a small tin.
7. There was a very good glaze on the china.
8. The workmen glazed every window in the house.
9. Brussel sprouts are out of season in May.
10. The cook had to season the food with salt, pepper and herbs.
11. The manager went to London on official business.
12. Dan used to be a professional player but now he acts as an official at matches.

Syllables

In dictionaries the separate syllables of words are shown by placing dashes between syllables.

A Write out the following words and separate their syllables by dashes. For example, (a) *behind* be-hind (b) *delicate* del-i-cate (c) *plantation* plan-ta-tion. (You may need your dictionary to help you.) The first one is done for you.

1. bargain (*Answer* bar-gain)
2. blossom
3. canoe
4. children
5. company
6. direct
7. equator
8. everlasting
9. express
10. fatigue
11. fiddle
12. fixture
13. foreign
14. harmony
15. hyacinth
16. knowledge
17. negro
18. nuisance
19. ornament
20. paragraph
21. strawberry
22. treasure
23. tweezers
24. unavoidable

Accent

It is helpful to know which syllable to accent. The dictionary tells you this as well by using the symbol '. This symbol is placed immediately after the syllable you must accent. For example:
(a) *dinner* (din'-er); *comrade* (kum'-rad).
    The accent falls on the first syllable.
(b) *consult* (kon-sult'); *disrupt* (dis-rupt'); *dispose* (dis-pos').
    The accent falls on the second syllable.

A Copy down each of the following words and its pronunciation. Put in the sign ' to show which syllable should be accented. The first one is done for you.

1. ornament (*Answer* or'-na-ment)
2. autumn (au-tum)
3. convent (con-vent)
4. dinner (din-er)
5. maintain (main-tain)
6. advance (ad-vans)
7. bargain (bar-gin)
8. double (dub-l)
9. follow (fol-o)
10. replay (re-pla)
11. encounter (en-kount-er)
12. electric (e-lek-trik)
13. satisfy (sat-is-fy)
14. dinosaur (di-no-sawr)

In many words, the accent may fall on different syllables, depending on the way the word is being used.
For example: (a) object (ob-jekt') (b) object (ob'-jekt)
The word is spelt the same in each case but note that the accent does not fall on the same syllable each time.
(a) object (ob-jekt') *v.* to protest against.
     David wanted to object about the price of sweets.
(b) object (ob'-jekt) means a material thing.
     Kala saw a strange-looking object in the wood.

B Copy out each word (1(a) to 5(b)) and its pronunciation. Put in the sign to show which syllable is accented when the word is used as in the sentence that follows.
For example: content (kon-tent) She was quite content to let the matter rest.
     Answer: content (kon-tent').

1. (a) alternate (al-ter-nat) Marion watched television on alternate evenings.

   (b) alternate (al-ter-nat) The headmaster decided to alternate the musical items and plays in the school concert.

2. (a) subject (sub-jekt) It was not fair to subject the passengers to such delay.

   (b) subject (sub-jekt) The pupils were given no choice of subject for their essay.

3. (a) extract (eks-strakt) Duncan asked the dentist to extract one tooth.

   (b) extract (eks-strakt) Jean cut out an extract from the magazine.

40

4. (a) protest (pro-test) All the people in the
street signed a <u>protest</u>
about noise from the
factory.

  (b) protest (pro-test) Customers were told to
<u>protest</u> to the manager
in person if they were
not satisfied.

5. (a) perfect (per-fekt) The weather was
<u>perfect</u> for a picnic.

  (b) perfect (per-fekt) The tennis player tried
to <u>perfect</u> his serving
techniques.

Pronunciation

As well as giving you the separate syllables, your dictionary
gives you the pronunciation of each one. At the foot of each
page of Collin's New English Dictionary we read, "fāte, fȧr, ạdo;
mē, hẹr; mīte; nōte; mȯȯn; tūne." This explains that the symbol
 ā is pronounced as in *fate*
 ȧ is pronounced as in *far*
 ē is pronounced as in *me*, etc.

A The following words are copied from the dictionary giving
the syllables and pronunciation of each one. Write out in
your own book the correct spelling of each of the following.
(Example: me-kan'-ik mechanic)

1. bē-lēv'	6. dē-send'	11. nō'-tis	16. res'-tor-ant
2. bus'-l	7. dē-skrīb'	12. sav-āj'	17. koun'-sil
3. kam'-e-rạ	8. en-dūr'	13. shuv'-l	18. mos-kē'-tō
4. Kris'-mạs	9. grān	14. dis-kuv'-er	
5. kol'-um	10. ū'-mur	15. nash'-un-al	

Origins of Words

Where did the words in our language come from? The dictionary
should give you this information. When we know the origin of a
word it helps us to remember what it means.
For example: school *n.* an institution for teaching boys or girls or
    both; *v.* to educate (Gk. *schole*, place for
    discussion).
The information in brackets tells us that school comes from the
Greek word *schole*, which means a place for discussion.

A Find out from your dictionary the origin of each word underlined, and what it means.

Example James saw the animals in the zoo.

  Answer: Zoo from Greek *zoon*, meaning animal.

1. The first thing he learned at school was the alphabet. (Answer Alphabet from *alpha* and *beta*, the first two letters of the Greek alphabet.)
2. Dynamite was used to blow up the building.
3. The bird watcher saw an eagle hovering above the valley.
4. No one was allowed to enter through the exit.
5. Mary had to learn the grammar so that she could speak the language.
6. The meat had been cooked under the grill.
7. The tennis player had a pain in his elbow joint.
8. The secretary could not read the writing; it was not legible.
9. The pupils carried out the experiments in the laboratory.
10. The manager had to take all the major decisions himself.
11. The question of taxes was debated in parliament.
12. Koyo had marmalade and toast for breakfast.
13. The knight felt his face was unprotected as he had no visor.

B Use your dictionary (and encyclopedia if necessary) to find the origin of each word underlined.

Example James played rugby for his school.

  Answer: rugby from Rugby public school where the game was first played.

1. The duke rode in a brougham at the transport exhibition.
2. In the cold weather Graham wore a balaclava to protect his ears from the cold.
3. Tracey's cardigan was hand knitted.
4. The forsythia was in full bloom in early April.
5. The murderer was put to death by guillotine.
6. The playground was surfaced with tar-macadam.
7. The children wore their mackintoshes on rainy days.
8. He wore a stetson as a protection from the very bright sun.
9. The reading lamp had a 100 watt bulb.
10. His wellingtons kept his feet dry as he walked through the puddle.

4. Figurative Language

A writer often uses figurative language so that he may make his writing more exciting and more memorable and he may thus succeed in making his meaning more vivid and more picturesque to the reader.

Simile

One of the most common figures of speech is the *simile*. For example:

(a) Mary was like a fish out of water on her first day at her new school.
   (She was not like a fish out of water at all. But the expression gives us the idea that she felt very much out of place.)

(b) The surface of the sea was like a mirror.
   (Again we do not mean the sea actually looked like a mirror. But we can see in our minds what the surface may have looked like.)

A Rewrite the following sentences in a way which will show what they mean literally. You will need to write a literal expression in place of the figurative one underlined each time.

1. Tom was <u>as busy as a bee</u> all day.
2. The old lady was <u>as deaf as a post</u>.
3. The sprinter was <u>as fast as a deer</u>.
4. In the dangerous situation, when all others were terrified, Charles was <u>as cool as a cucumber</u>.

B Rewrite each sentence. For each figurative expression underlined, substitute another figurative expression which will give the same meaning.

1. When Arnold won the weight-lifting competition, everyone realised that he was <u>as strong as an ox</u>.

2. Whenever he got out to the river to fish, Shoji was as happy as a sandboy.
3. Jean thought that the books in the museum were as old as Methuselah.
4. When Lilian explained to her father how to translate the manuscript, he told her she was as wise as Solomon.
5. After long exposure to the sea and sun, Jenny's face was as red as a beetroot.

C   Complete each sentence with a suitable figurative expression. A suggested answer is given for the first one.
   1. The epidemic spread like _____.
      (*Answer* The epidemic spread like underline wildfire.)
   2. The second-hand books sold like _____ at the sale.
   3. The people in the crowd were packed together like _____.
   4. Mr Adams objected strongly to blood sports. To him even the mention of the word *hunt* was like _____.
   5. Anne ignored everyone's advice. Any suggestion made to her was just like _____.

Metaphor

A metaphor is a comparison where we say one thing *is* another; but in the strictly literal sense it is not true. For example:
(a) Mr Williams is a queer fish.
      (He is not literally a fish at all. He is a person with odd habits.)
(b) On her first day in the Air Force, Jan was a very small fish in a very large pond.

A   Rewrite each sentence, putting in a literal expression in place of the metaphor underlined. The first one has been done for you.
   1. The tea had been simmering so long that it was plain tar.
      (*Answer* The tea had been simmering so long that it was very dark in colour.)
   2. Nancy was storing up every idea she could get from anyone else. She had always been a squirrel.
   3. The teacher thought her new class was the best she had ever had. Every pupil was golden.
   4. The centre-half was a rock in the team's defence.
   5. George's back was poker stiff.
   6. The voyage in the liner was very enjoyable. The sea was a mill pond all the way.
   7. With the sun shining on the surrounding area the lake was a picture.

44

8. The foreman <u>bellowed</u> to his men to start work immediately.
9. The Member of Parliament was <u>poleaxed</u> when he saw the number of votes he had lost in the election.
10 The lawyer tried to get the whole story out of Reginald but he was <u>too slippery an eel</u> to be persuaded to give full answers to all the questions.

Pun

A pun is a humorous play on words having a similar sound but different meanings.
For example: A heading in a newspaper reads, "Write is wrong".
It is a catching headline because we think of *right* (with the same pronunciation as *write*) as being the opposite of *wrong*. The article in the newspaper went on to say that the writer's wife thought it wrong for him to undertake to write another book.

A Below are twelve headlines we might see in newspapers and the beginning of each article. Find and explain the pun in each case.

1. <u>Fair deal demanded</u>
   Bus passengers marched on the transport offices and asked for cheaper fares.
   (*Answer Fare* and *fair* have the same pronunciation. *Fare* is the price a passenger pays. *Fair* means just.)

2. <u>Grave offence</u>
   Dan Roberts was jailed for two months for knocking over gravestones in the cemetery and causing thousands of pounds worth of damage . . .

3. <u>The bell told his presence</u>
   A burglar was arrested in the church after a bell tolled mysteriously. It appeared that he had accidentally stepped upon a bell rope . . .

4. <u>A cheap sail</u>
   In the sale on the last day of the boat show all dinghies were sold off at knock down prices . . .

5. <u>Plain food not acceptable</u>
   The survey showed that the food provided for flight passengers was not of a high standard and certainly not good enough for a modern plane . . .

6. <u>Nerves of steel</u>
   The judge was amazed at the prisoner's nerve when he tried to steal the jewels . . .

7. The key to success
   The government has agreed that the industry will die off unless a new quay is built quickly . . .

8. A day of rain
   The gala queen's one day reign was marred by wet and windy weather from dawn to dusk . . .

9. A great heat
   Mr Alan has solved the problem of poor heating in the drawing room of the old mansion house. He has opened up the eighteenth-century grate . . .

10. £5000 to remove from sight
    The Council is willing to pay £5000 to a contractor to demolish the property at Hillview as the site on which it stands would be valuable for new development . . .

11. Still hire prices
    The attempts to abolish day rates for use of deck-chairs was defeated at the Local Council. Another motion was passed which in fact means higher rates . . .

12. No monkey business will be allowed
    Radlys have been refused a licence to sell African monkeys. The manager was warned against trying to start up any such venture in future without going through the proper authorities.

Idioms

An idiom is an expression whose meaning cannot be understood from the literal meanings of the words used.
Example The boys had all agreed to tell no one but it was now clear that one of them had let the cat out of the bag.
Let the cat out of the bag means to disclose something that was secret or confidential.

A Rewrite each sentence in the following exercise and for the idiom underlined substitute a suitable phrase from the list at the end of the exercise.
   1. The soldier had had no promotion in twenty years and there seemed to be no prospect in the year ahead. He could not understand why he was in the doldrums.
   2. James knew that he had been seen by at least four passers-by and had been identified. He would just have to face the music.

3. When Graeme failed in his business, not one of his relations was surprised. He had always been the black sheep of the family.
4. Mr Smith had his taxes increased, his salary reduced and his car withdrawn, but he decided the increase in working hours was the last straw.
5. Ann knew that there was no chance of being allowed time off but she decided she would take French leave so that she could watch the procession.
6. The car broke down on the third day after David bought it and he was astounded to hear that it was not worth repairing. Never again would he buy a pig in a poke.
7. No one at the chicken farm would buy eggs from Jack Muir. Farmer Brown pointed out to him that there was no point in bringing coals to Newcastle.
8. Janis pretended to be very sorry and she shed crocodile tears when George told her of his misfortune.
9. Greta looked a very promising hockey player when she scored five times in her very first match, but alas, it was only a flash in the pan.

Phrases
(a) go without permission
(b) too much to bear
(c) was insincere
(d) accept the consequences
(e) making no progress
(f) taking something to a place where there is already plenty
(g) a blind bargain
(h) a good show at the beginning without accomplishing anything
(i) one who lets down his relations

B   Rewrite the following short passage. Substitute for each idiom underlined a phrase which gives the literal meaning.

Redford had always been one to blow his own trumpet. For years we had listened to his tales about his bravery in his wartime exploits, but when Alex discovered his real age we all began to smell a rat. We started to make a few quiet investigations.

When Redford discovered that we had been able to see his wartime record he did in fact hang his head. He realised that he might as well make a clean breast of it and admit he had told us many tall stories. He hoped that we would all be friends again and that none of us would give him the cold shoulder.

5. Words and Pictures

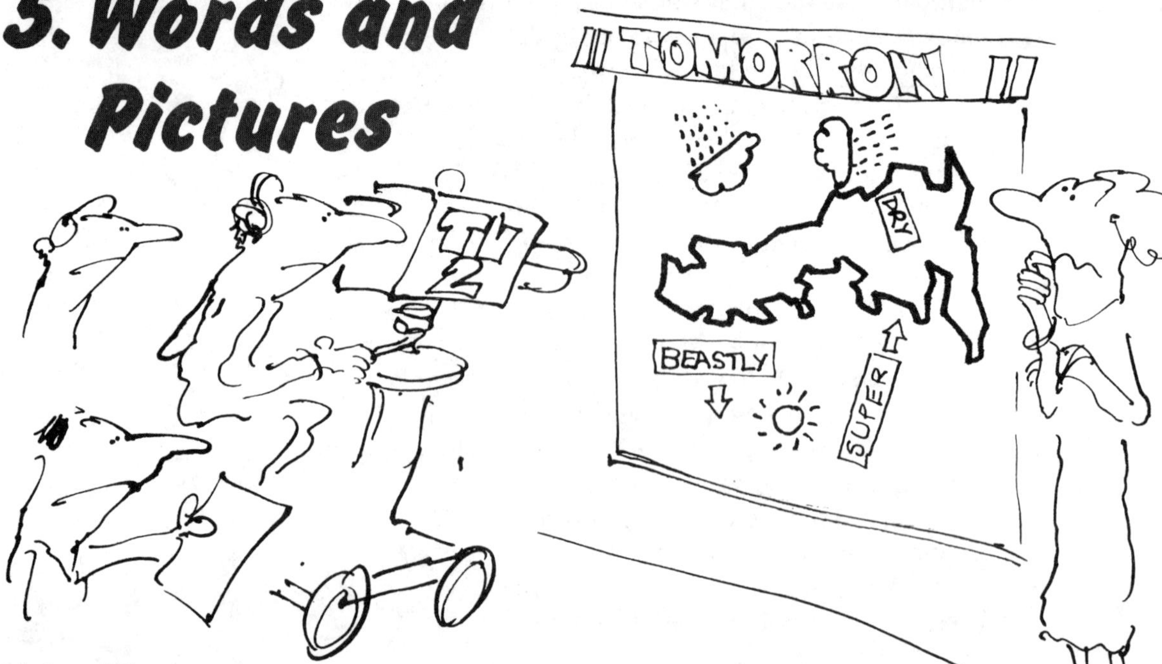
TOMORROW
TV 2
DRY
BEASTLY
SUPER

Using Diagrams

Often information and instructions are given clearly in diagrams, with very few words or even no words at all.

Assemble Your Cold Frame

Check that you have:

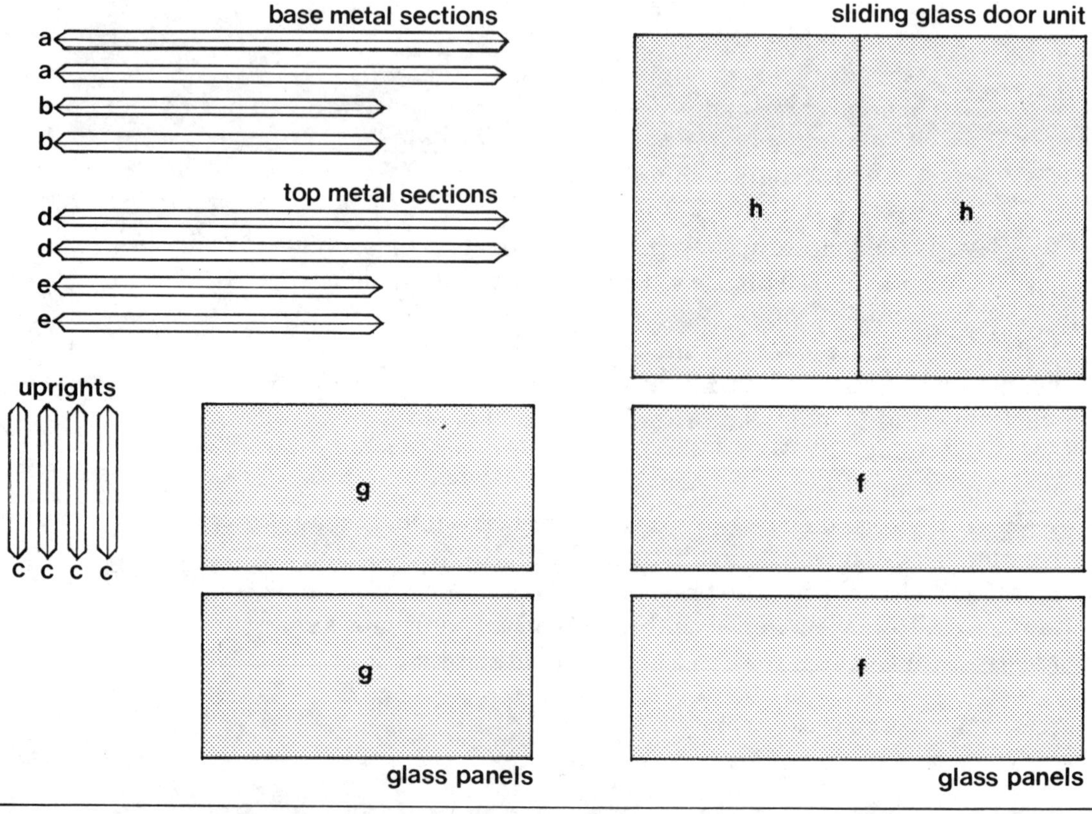
base metal sections
a
a
b
b
top metal sections
d
d
e
e
uprights
c c c c
sliding glass door unit
h
h
g
g
glass panels
f
f
glass panels

A   The assembly instructions are given in diagrammatic form.
Supply a written instruction to go with each diagram.

For example:

1. Connect together the 4 base metal sections, placing the long sections opposite each other and likewise the short sections opposite each other.

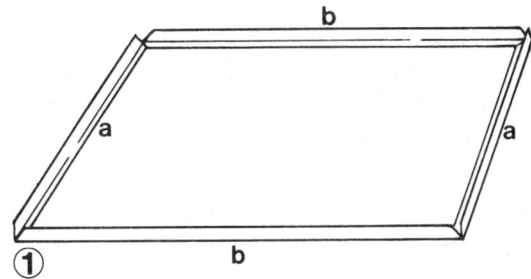

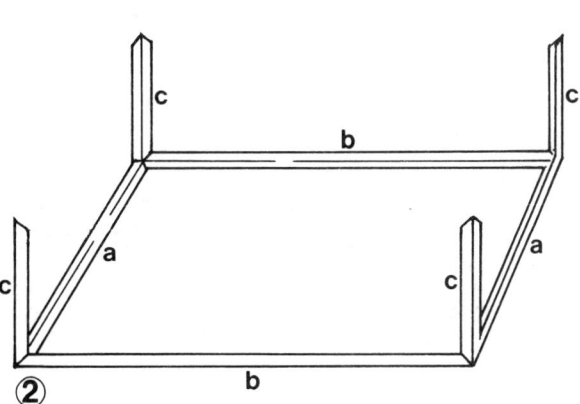

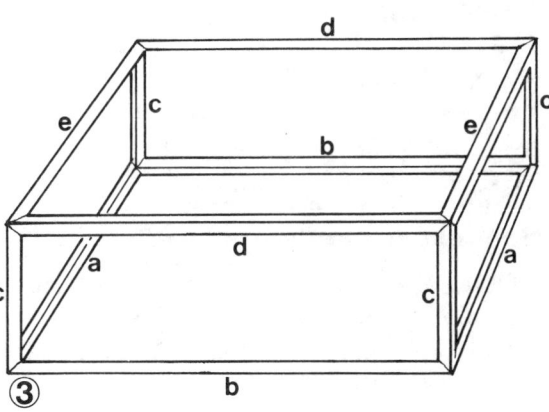

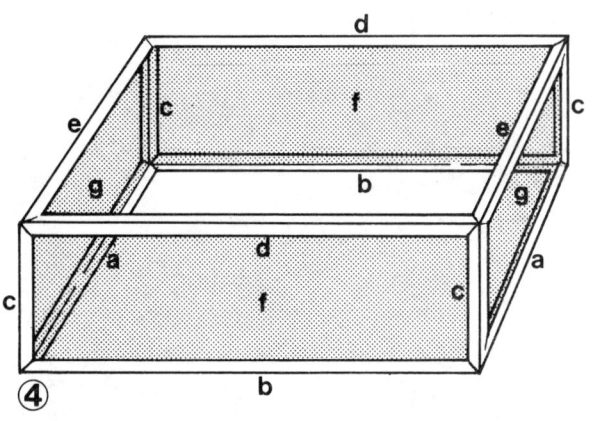

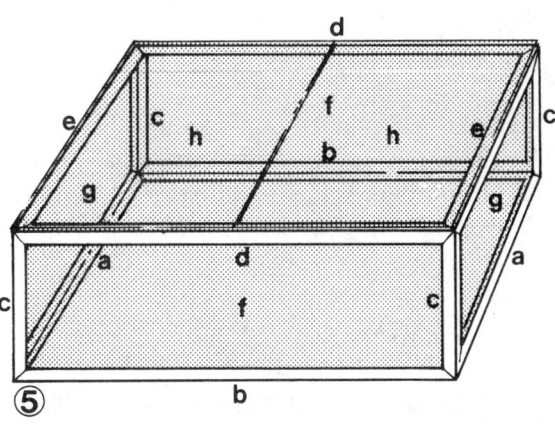

MAKE YOUR OWN TOBOGGAN

If you want to make this toboggan, don't wait until the snow has started to fall because it might have melted by the time you have finished making it! You should be able to get the metal runners made up by a metal-working firm or blacksmith.

MATERIALS
Two pieces of softwood 90 cm × 15 cm × 3 cm, planed, for sides.
Two pieces of square softwood 70 cm × 5 cm × 5 cm, planed, for bracers.
Seven pieces of softwood 40 cm × 7 cm × 3 cm, planed, for cross-pieces.
Twenty-six 30 mm no. 10 screws.
50 mm oval nails.
210 cm length of 12 mm rope.
Two 110 cm lengths of metal strip 35 mm × 5 mm, with holes drilled at 10 cm intervals, starting 2 cm from the end. These holes should be countersunk and the right size to take a 25 mm no. 8 screw.
Twenty 25 mm no. 8 screws.
Sandpaper, varnish, glue.

TOOLS
60 cm folding rule, 30 cm steel rule, try square, pencil, saw, hammer, rasp and file, screwdriver, two G cramps, drill and 12 mm bit.

(Harwood *My Fun with Wood Book*)

On the opposite page the ten steps in making the toboggan are shown. The steps are described by means of diagrams. Some diagrams have no written instructions and others have part of the instructions only.

B Make up complete instructions to accompany each diagram. (Numbers 1, 2, 5 and 6 are done for you.)
    1. Cut the necessary pieces of wood to the sizes shown here.
    2. Make template as shown.
    3. (Make up instruction.)
    4. (Make up instruction.)
    5. (Copy down the instruction given.)
    6. (Copy down the instruction given.)
    7. (Fill in the missing parts of the instructions.)
    8. (Fill in the missing parts of the instructions.)
    9. (Copy down the instruction given.)
    10. (Fill in the missing parts of the instructions.)

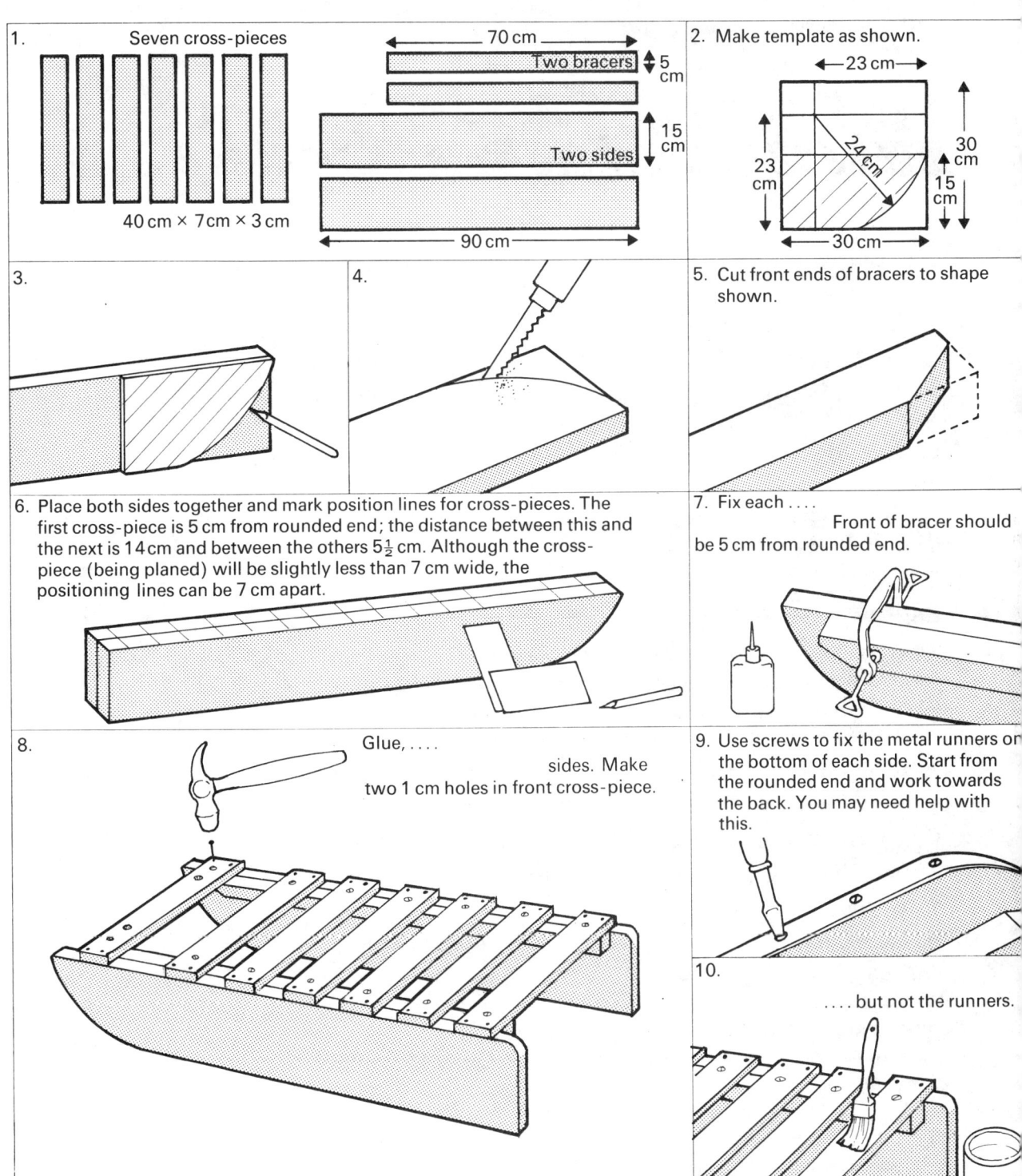

1. Seven cross-pieces

40 cm × 7 cm × 3 cm

70 cm

Two bracers — 5 cm

15 cm

Two sides

90 cm

2. Make template as shown.

23 cm

23 cm

24 cm

30 cm

15 cm

30 cm

3.

4.

5. Cut front ends of bracers to shape shown.

6. Place both sides together and mark position lines for cross-pieces. The first cross-piece is 5 cm from rounded end; the distance between this and the next is 14 cm and between the others 5½ cm. Although the cross-piece (being planed) will be slightly less than 7 cm wide, the positioning lines can be 7 cm apart.

7. Fix each . . . .

Front of bracer should be 5 cm from rounded end.

8.

Glue, ...

sides. Make two 1 cm holes in front cross-piece.

9. Use screws to fix the metal runners on the bottom of each side. Start from the rounded end and work towards the back. You may need help with this.

10.

. . . . but not the runners.

Assignment

Make up a set of diagrams and instructions for something you may have to do yourself, eg. changing torch batteries, covering a book.

SECTION D
What's The Point?

6. Main Ideas

Reducing Sentences

When we are taking notes we do not copy whole sentences or paragraphs. We might reduce some of the sentences from the text we are studying. We can do this by keeping only the few important words which capture the main idea and still give the meaning of the sentence.

Example sentence	*Sentence reduced*
The village of Portmeirion on the Welsh coast is famous for its beautiful botanic gardens.	Portmeirion famous for beautiful botanic gardens.
Nearly 12 000 people in different parts of England and Wales were affected by various kinds of food poisoning over the course of last year.	Nearly 12 000 in England and Wales affected by food poisoning last year.

A Identify the main idea in the following sentences and reduce each sentence to a few words.
1. It would be very difficult to carry eight adults or children in a small vehicle.
2. The passengers might have luggage as well which would require quite a lot of room.
3. What you need is an eight-seater car with a good-sized luggage space.

4. It is important that everyone in the car can sit and relax in comfort for the whole journey.
5. Most cars are not built to carry such a large number of passengers and luggage in addition.

B Identify the main idea in the following sentences and reduce each sentence to a few words.

Example sentence
Some parts of the world which we have never visited have very much the same type of weather the whole year through.

Sentence reduced
some parts of world with same weather all year.

1. Near the North Pole and South Pole it is always very cold with snow and ice covering everything.
2. In many areas near the Equator it is always very hot.
3. In Great Britain the weather is changeable and we notice the changes from season to season.
4. We think of Spring as the first season of the year but it does not begin in January.
5. Our warmest time of the year is in the summer months which are June, July and August.
6. School children look forward to the summer because they have a long break from school.
7. It is at this time of year that many of them get away for a holiday somewhere in Britain or abroad.
8. In winter the days are short and it is often cold.
9. Children enjoy cold spells with snow and ice so that they can take part in such sports as sledging and ski-ing.
10. In Australia they have summer when we have winter because seasons occur at opposite times to ours.

C Identify the main idea and reduce each sentence to a few words. The first one has been done for you.
1. A famous Carthaginian general, called Hamilcar, began preparing for a new war.
   (*Answer* Hamilcar preparing for new war.)

2. He asked his son Hannibal to swear that he would always be an enemy of Rome.
3. The boy agreed eagerly and he kept this promise for the rest of his life.
4. Hannibal trained as a soldier so that he could fight against Rome.
5. He then went with his father to fight in a war in Spain.
6. There he quickly learned to be a good and skilful leader.

7. When his father was killed in battle Hannibal was made the new leader of the Carthaginian army in Spain.
8. Immediately he began to think of how he could defeat the Romans who now had strong armies and strong fleets.
9. The best chance, he decided, would be to conquer the city of Rome itself.
10. He would not go by sea as he might be defeated by the Roman ships.
11. He would go by land which meant marching through France and then crossing the high mountain ranges called the Alps.
12. Many of the men despaired at the sight of the great mountains they had to cross.
13. They were soon exhausted as they climbed the narrow and steep paths.
14. In the ice and snow they suffered terribly from cold and they were very hungry as food was very short.
15. Local people rolled down stones which was very dangerous.
16. Avalanches of snow and ice swept men over the cliffs and ice faces.
17. Only about half of Hannibal's army arrived weary and starving at the Roman side of the Alps.
18. But the Romans were in panic when they heard the news that Hannibal and his army were in Italy.

Paragraphs

A Read each paragraph and write out what each paragraph is mainly about. (Choose what you think is best from the suggestions given.)

1. As Anne was lazing in the sun on the upper deck she noticed a dark triangular fin coming in the direction of the ship. This, said Edmund, was a killer whale of the type she had been reading about. As it came nearer she could see that the upper parts of the head and body were black, and, as it turned to change course, she caught a glimpse of the white underneath. It was not close enough for her to make out clearly the short snout and rounded head.

Paragraph 1 is mainly about (a) Anne lazing in the sun
                               (b) what the killer whale looks like
                               (c) the whale's rounded head

2. She had been interested to read that killer whales might be seen in any of the Oceans and certainly they might be sighted from time to time in the Atlantic. Their ship was still in the Atlantic although nearing the coast of Spain.
   Paragraph 2 is mainly about (a) the coast of Spain
                                      (b) where the killer whale might be sighted

3. An hour later Anne observed black fins close together. She guessed that a number of killer whales had come together to hunt for she knew that they hunt in packs. She shuddered as she thought of the group together attacking their prey with their murderous teeth.
   Paragraph 3 is mainly about (a) black fins
                                      (b) whales' teeth
                                      (c) how killer whales hunt

4. Everything that lives in the sea is terrified of the killer whale. Not only small fish, but even dolphins, sea-lions, seals and other types of whales will rush to escape. Seals and sea-lions in their terror will try to get up on to the rocks for safety. Dolphins' fright can be so great that they will throw themselves into shallow water where they hope the killer whale cannot follow.
   Paragraph 4 is mainly about (a) seals trying to escape on to the rocks
                                      (b) everything that lives in the sea fleeing to escape
                                      (c) dolphins throwing themselves into shallows

5. But Anne knew that they would not all escape. Together the pack would attack a victim and kill it. With their powerful teeth they would tear off mouthfuls of flesh and swim away to swallow them. No sooner than each had finished a mouthful it would hurry back for more and more until the carcass would be finished.
   Paragraph 5 is mainly about (a) how the carcass would be eaten up
                                      (b) the teeth of the killer whale

6. Anne was sure that the ship had not frightened the killer whales. They did not seem to be frightened of ships at all. They have been known to come close to whaling ships and to bite mouthfuls of flesh from whales being towed by the whalers.
   Paragraph 6 is mainly about (a) killer whales not being afraid of ships
                                      (b) killer whales biting flesh from whales

B Make up a label, headline or sub-heading for each numbered paragraph below.

1. Leon Roper's hopes were high when he arrived at Westchester City Hall on 20 April, 1988. Success might only be three weeks away when he was to be given a test for a place in the Philharmonic Orchestra.

2. Immediately after his arrival at the City Hall he took out his cello to practice Saint Saens' "The Swan". He practised for hours as he wished to be note perfect. He knew he must play extremely well if he was to be chosen.

3. At lunch time he locked away his cello in the rehearsal room. There it would be safe and out of harm's way, or at least so he thought.

4. While he was away the central heating system had gone out of control. When he returned, Leon found his cello half-baked. The heat had twisted the wood out of shape and shrivelled up the strings.

5. Three days later a claim reached General Union, the Assurance Company through which he had insured the instrument. The company decided that the simplest and quickest answer was to give Leon a new cello to replace the old one.

6. But Leon had other ideas. He wrote to say that to be without his normal instrument could cause him a great deal of worry. He did not feel the same without it. It was of more value to him than any other he could get to replace it.

7. General Union immediately set about repairs. They found experts who would be able to do the job. At the Assurance Company's expense Leon Roper and his cello were taken to London, so that the work could be done quickly. A week later he returned to audition for Westchester Philharmonic.

8. How fortunate for him that he was insured with the General Union!

In the passage opposite the writer tries to describe the scene and the atmosphere for us. The seven paragraphs deal with (a) to (g) below.

C Which paragraph deals with:
   (a) a scene of horror and excitement (*Answer* paragraph 1)
   (b) sounds heard while waiting anxiously (*Answer* paragraph 6)
   (c) a scene of confusion
   (d) taking firm action
   (e) fear of something about to happen
   (f) a scene of destruction
   (g) uncertainty of how to act.

Air Raid

1. Brian's heart seemed to be thumping as loudly as the guns. He watched fascinated and horrified as the plane came nearer. The ack-ack was bombarding it furiously. Between the thumps of the guns, he could hear the drone of the aircraft's engines. The note wavered slightly as the sound travelled to him through the night air.

2. Suddenly there was a flash, followed by the bang of an explosion. Spurts of flame shot from the wing. Or was it the engine? Brian couldn't be sure. He heard a series of small, sharp explosions, like a car engine backfiring several times in quick succession. Then the engine went up in a sheet of flame. For a second, Brian couldn't see the plane or the flames coming from it, but then, as the fuel tanks ruptured and exploded, a great burst of fire surged into the sky. The first brightness gradually subsided into lesser flames which flickered beneath an immense pall of dense smoke.

3. Against the confusion of flame and cloud and smoke and moon, Brian saw – he was almost certain he saw – a parachute. A parachute drifting down the wind, much closer to Uncle Arthur's farm than the wrecked plane. Just for a second. Then it was lost in the darkness.

4. He crept back to his bedroom. He checked that the window-catch was securely fastened. He didn't have a key to his bedroom door, so he jammed a chair under the door-handle. He glanced nervously at the chimney. There wasn't anything he could do about *that*.

5. Then he lay down on his bed and took a firm hold on his sheath-knife, under the pillow. He wondered what he should do. He wished Andy was around. Andy would know what would be best.

6. He heard a distant siren sound the all-clear. The breeze whispered in the leaves of the big cherry tree. Occasionally the sash window, tugged and pushed by the wind, gave a little double rattle in its frame.

7. This was what Brian had hoped for, and feared, for years. His chance to meet a real enemy. For over an hour, rigid with fear, he lay there. He kept his eyes tightly closed, not daring to look at the pale rectangle of the window, for fear that he might suddenly see outlined there the head and shoulders of the enemy parachutist.

(Spooner *Rainbow Cake*)

D Write down the details the writer uses to convey the main thought in each paragraph. For example:

Paragraph 1: A scene of horror and excitement

> *Details:* (a) ack-ack guns fired at approaching plane

        (b) sounds of shots and of plane's
              engines
        (c) sound of engines wavering

E   After reading the passage on pages 58–60 about
     the *Titanic* suggest:
    1. reasons why people considered the *Titanic* almost
       unsinkable;
    2. arguments which might have been used by Captain
       Smith for proceeding at $22\frac{1}{2}$ knots in spite of the
       warnings of ice;
    3. arguments some passengers might have put forward for
       not being alarmed (at first) when told of the collision
       with an iceberg.
    4. reasons why it seemed so long between Fleet's warning
       of the iceberg ahead and the ship's swing to port.

F   At the end there is the type of SOS message the *Titanic*
    might have sent out. Notice that as few words as possible
    are included.
       Suppose you were a reporter on board and had the
    opportunity to send a signal message for inclusion in the
    stop press of a newspaper about the events described in the
    passage, you would send only important pieces of
    information using as few words as possible.
       Your message might begin "*Titanic* travelling at $22\frac{1}{2}$
    knots . . ." Complete the message in your own way.
       From which paragraphs would you not take any
    information for your very important message? Why not?

Unsinkable

1. It was indeed a special event which brought spectators
   thronging to the docks at Southampton on 10 April, 1912.
   They had come to witness the noon departure of the White
   Star liner, *Titanic*, setting out on her maiden voyage.
2. This, the largest and most luxurious vessel afloat, was
   being hailed as almost unsinkable. To protect her against
   any unforeseen emergency she had a double bottom and
   sixteen watertight compartments. Any of these compartments found to be taking in water could be sealed off by
   watertight doors operated automatically from the bridge,
   thus enabling the ship to stay afloat. In every aspect the
   ship was very advanced in design.
3. To be on board felt like being in a floating town. There were
   cabins, state rooms, dining rooms, cafés, reading rooms,
   smoking rooms, shops, gymnasium and swimming baths.

This luxurious ship did not only look safe; one felt safe within its massive structure.

4. After her triumphant departure from Southampton she stopped at Cherbourg, France, and then at Queenstown, Ireland, for mail and passengers. Now with over 2200 people aboard the *Titanic* set course for New York.

5. The evening of 14 April 1912, found her proceeding westward at $22\frac{1}{2}$ knots in unbelievably calm Atlantic waters. Visibility was good, the star-laden sky was clear and the steady quiet rhythm of the engines had a soothing and reassuring effect.

6. Some hours earlier the German steamer, *Amerika*, had reported by radio telegraph to Captain F. J. Smith of the *Titanic* that it had passed two icebergs. Although no one could foretell it then, the reported position of the icebergs was only $12\frac{1}{2}$ miles from where the Titanic's voyage would end. The French liner, *La Touraine*, had also sent messages about the presence of icebergs. Captain Smith's reaction to these warnings seems to have been to order the men in the crow's nest to keep a sharp lookout for ice. He did not alter course nor reduce speed.

7. Suddenly at 11.39 approximately Frederick Fleet, high up in the crow's nest, saw directly in the ship's path what he later described as a 'small black mass' about the size of two table tops. Within seconds he realised the ship was on collision course with a mass of ice of monstrous size. On the crow's nest telephone he immediately rang the bridge to report 'Iceberg right ahead'.

8. For what seemed to him a long time Fleet watched the ship race towards the ice. Just when a head-on crash seemed inevitable the bows began to swing to port and almost clear the berg. As he braced himself for the collision the berg seemed to brush along the starboard side of the ship depositing ice on the deck as it went. In a matter of seconds it was gone and had disappeared into the night. A narrow shave, thought Fleet.

9. Fleet was not alone in underestimating the seriousness of the position. Some passengers were aware of a large object passing along the side of the ship; some had identified it as a gigantic iceberg but it had vanished as quickly as it had appeared and they felt hardly any impact at all and many had no idea what had happened. Even when the rumour buzzed round the ship that it had hit an iceberg, the majority of passengers showed no sign of alarm.

10. In the second class smoke room there was discussion about the liner brushing against an iceberg, but it did not seem to be cause for any real concern. One man is quoted as having said to his companion, "Just run along the deck and see if

59

any ice has come aboard. I would like some for this". He was referring to the whisky glass he was holding.

11. Captain Smith who was in his cabin at the time of the collision, rushed to the bridge when he felt the impact. All too soon, and to his horror, he was to learn that the iceberg had torn a hundred metre gash in the ship's side below the waterline. Before long he would order lifeboats to be launched and instruct the telegraphist to send out SOS messages for urgent help.

The type of SOS message the Titanic *might have sent out*

```
00.17   15 APRIL    SOS    HAVE  STRUCK  ICEBERG.

 SINKING  FAST.    REQUIRE  IMMEDIATE  ASSISTANCE.

POSITION:  LATITUDE 41.46N   LONGITUDE 50.14 WEST.

                                      TITANIC
```

Summary

* Make an outline of the following story. Note a few details under each heading.
    1. Mama's accusation against the Wallaces.
    2. The opinion of Mama and her friends of the Wallaces.
    3. The action Mama asked to be taken against the Wallaces.
    4. Why people would not boycott the Wallaces.

Convert your outline into a summary by writing it out in a few sentences. Here is a beginning:

Outline
1. *Mama's accusation against the Wallaces.*
    (a) poured kerosene over Mr Berry and his nephews
    (b) lit the kerosene
    (c) killed one nephew, injured Mr Berry and the other nephew.

* If more introductory work is required on outlines and summaries, see *Directions 2* (page 38) and *More Directions 1* (page 55).

2. *Opinion Mama and her friends had of the Wallaces.*
   (a) bad people
   (b)
   (c)

Fair Deal

After we were on the main road again, having ridden in thoughtful silence over the wooded trail, Mama said quietly, "The Wallaces did that, children. They poured kerosene over Mr. Berry and his nephews and lit them afire. One of the newphews died, the other one is just like Mr. Berry." She allowed this information to penetrate the silence, then went on. "Everyone knows they did it, and the Wallaces even laugh about it, but nothing was ever done. They're bad people, the Wallaces. That's why I don't want you to ever go to their store again – for any reason. You understand?"

We nodded, unable to speak as we thought of the disfigured man lying in the darkness.

On the way home we stopped at the homes of some of Mama's students, where families poured out of tenant shacks to greet us. At each farm Mama spoke of the bad influence of the Wallaces, of the smoking and drinking permitted at their store, and asked that the family's children not be allowed to go there.

The people nodded and said she was right.

She also spoke of finding another store to patronise, one where the proprietors were more concerned about the welfare of the community. But she did not speak directly of what the Wallaces had done to the Berrys for, as she explained later, that was something that wavered between the known and the unknown and to mention it outright to anyone outside of those with whom you were closest was not wise. There were too many ears that listened for others besides themselves, and too many tongues that wagged to those they shouldn't.

The people only nodded, and Mama left.

When we reached the Turner farm, Moe's widowed father rubbed his stubbled chin and squinted across the room at Mama. "Miz Logan," he said, "you know I feels the same way you do 'bout them low-down Wallaces, but it ain't easy to jus' stop shoppin' there. They overcharges me and I has to pay them high interest, but I gots credit there 'cause Mr. Montier signs for me. Now you know most folks 'round here sharecroppin' on Montier, Granger, or Harrison land and most of them jus' 'bout got to shop at that Wallace store or up at the mercantile in Strawberry, which is jus' 'bout as bad. Can't go no place else."

Mama nodded solemnly, showing she understood, then she said, "For the past year now, our family's been shopping down at Vicksburg. There are a number of stores down there and we've found several that treat us well."

"Vicksburg?" Mr. Turner echoed, shaking his head. "Lord, Miz Logan, you ain't expectin' me to go all the way to Vicksburg? That's an overnight journey in a wagon down there and back."

(Taylor Roll of Thunder Hear My Cry)

Assignments

1. *Work in a group of two or more. Each member of the group supplies a newspaper report (less than half a page) from home with the main headline and any other subheadings cut out. The other members of the group have to make up the missing headlines.*
2. *Look also at an interesting headline plus subheadings. Try to write the story to fit these headings.*

Make Up Your Own Questions

A Instead of writing answers to questions you are now going to make up questions which can be answered from the passage below. Try to avoid questions to which the answer is just simply yes or no. Begin your questions with words such as *when, where, why, how, who, what, which.*

You should have a question about each of the following:
1. The nature of Stewart's injuries.
2. Possible explanation of the cause of Stewart's injuries.
3. Corby's behaviour in school.
4. Corby's ability.
5. Corby's treatment of Stewart.
6. Corby's manner towards the Headmaster.

Ask another pupil to answer your questions from the story. Ask them to give reasons for their answers.

B See if you can make up two or three questions which interest you about this story but which are not answered in the passage. How would you find answers to these questions?

I am sitting by the side of a hospital bed watching Stewart trying to open a box of chocolates that Sir has brought him from me, if you get it. Stewpid is up on traction, which means his arm is up in the air, so that he can't lie down at all, even to sleep. If he moves it at all – the elbow, that is – it won't set properly, and he'll be no good at football, ever. I haven't seen him since they took him away, screaming his head off, with Jonathan Johns telling everybody gathered round that it was all my fault, bloomin' unfair because I can't help it if Pitt has the kind of bones that break easily, can I?

Afterwards I have to go to the Headmaster and explain to him that running off with the papermate was all a joke and could I help it if people had no sense of humour?

"I'm glad you've got such a good keen one, then," he says to me, twitching his bushy eyebrows, "because you're going to need it to see you through writing letters of apology to Stewart and his mother for the anguish and distress you've caused them. And, Gowie Corby, just listen to me –" here I sigh as deadly boredom hits me, I've heard it all before – "I know you have problems, but so have other people, you know. You're one of mine –" here he smiles as if making a joke – "so do try to be more co-operative in school, adopt a more positive approach" – now what's he burbling about, I wonder? – "and stop being so awkward. We are only here to help you." And that's a laugh for a start, I think, looking at a horrible plant on the window-sill. It could have come straight out of a Dr. Who programme. Suppose it grew suddenly and swallowed him up and everyone was runnning round looking for the missing Headmaster. "Corby, are you listening to me?"

"Yes, Sir."

"Well, as I said before and shall now repeat again, you are not without ability" – now just what does that mean? – "and you could do well in your last year here, if you settle down and buckle down to it."

"To what, Sir? I don't follow you."

"TO WORK, OF COURSE. AND GAMES. WHAT DO YOU THINK I MEAN?"

"Yes, Sir."

"Oh, go away, Corby. And let me see those letters when you've finished them."

"Can I go now?"

"Yes, I said so, didn't I?"

"Yes, Sir."

"Oh, remember to come to me if you have problems or difficulties."

"I don't have problems or difficulties. I just have enemies."

(Kemp *Gowie Corby Plays Chicken*)

Assignments

1. *Choose an extract not more than two pages long from a book you are reading. Make up five or six questions which will bring out the important points in this extract.*
2. *Make up one or two other questions to which you would like to know the answers.*
   Discuss with your friend how you might find the answers.

7. Linking Together

Writers use words and expressions that show how their thoughts are connected. One way they do this is by joining together separate sentences, using linking words which demonstrate that they are dealing with the same thought or idea.

Joining Words

A   Join the following pairs of related sentences using *who, whose, whom, which* or *that.*

1. Mabel paid back the money to her friend. From her she had received the loan. (*Answer* Mabel paid back the money to her friend from whom she had received the loan.)

2. Beside the main gate there was a mounted policeman. He was there to keep order in the queue if necessary.
3. In our class there is a new boy, Ramjan. His father was born in Pakistan.
4. Beside the road there was still the crane. It had been used to lift the car.
5. Mary went to see the new cottage. Jerry had built it entirely by himself.

Join the following pairs of sentences using other connecting words.

6. Fred brought his winter clothes with him to the outward-bound centre. He expected it to be very cold at that time of year.
7. The temperatures were reasonable during the day. At night it was invariably very, very cold.
8. This should not have surprised anyone. All knew that the January weather had been the same for the last five years.
9. He could not decide. Mountaineering might or might not be for him.
10. At last he came to the conclusion that he must participate in everything. He was hoping to prove to his friends that he was as good as anyone else.

Clues to What Follows

Instead of actually joining sentences together a writer may give clues as to what to expect in the sentence which is to follow. He may use clue words to warn us that more information is to be given.

Example The leader of the West Saxons in their battles against the Danes was a brave young king known as Alfred the Great. Moreover he is the only English king to be known as "the Great".

Moreover is the clue word that more information is to be given about the brave young king, Alfred.

A Read each of the following sentences and then complete the exercise on page 66:

1. Alfred was determined to prove that he knew how to lead his people successfully in war. Furthermore after a series of victories against the Danes he had shown that he could do so triumphantly.
2. He was determined to secure peace in his own kingdom. With this in view he set about bringing English law up to date so that it could be used to settle disputes.
3. Alfred and some of his friends collected laws from the Bible and from other kingdoms. In addition he sought the help of some learned priests who were knowledgeable about the laws of other countries.
4. Being anxious to ensure that every free-born boy should learn to read English, he decided to have educational Latin books translated into English. Further he often did the translating himself.
5. We find an example of this in the case of a Spanish history book; he translated it himself. As well as translating it he added a story about Othene, a Norse merchant, voyaging in the North Sea.
6. To strengthen defences against further Danish attacks he built strong forts in southern England. Besides this he built warships to help to defend his kingdom from attacks by sea.
7. Historians are grateful to Alfred because he began the *Anglo-Saxon Chronicle* which records the early history of England. It also gives us a picture of life in England in the ninth century.

(Grant *Children's History of Britain* adapted)

Write out and complete the following table in your own book.

Section	Clue words	More information to be given about
Example	moreover	the brave young king Alfred
1.	furthermore	proving his leadership
2.		
3.	in addition	his determination to secure peace
4.		
5.		
6.		
7.		

Contrasting thoughts

As we read we may recognise a thought that the writer is expressing. There are some words which give us a clue that he may be about to present a contrasting thought.

Example
James always liked to travel by train in spite of the fact that he could have saved much time by going by air.

First thought	Clue word(s) that there is to be a contrasting thought	Contrasting thought
James always liked to travel by train.	in spite of the fact that	he could have saved time by going by air.

Exercise

A For paragraphs numbered 1 to 8 below write out the first thought the writer expressed, the clue word (or words) warning us that a contrasting thought is coming, and the contrasting thought itself (as in the example above).

Games and sports

As leisure began to increase last century, many pastimes, games and sports were developed in various parts of the country.

1. Fishing had always attracted rich and poor alike but a poor person who could not make his own rod and tackle would not usually have been able to take part.

2. Cock-fighting is now looked on as a very cruel form of sport. Nonetheless over a hundred years ago it was thought to be highly exciting and many flocked to watch.
3. Shooting became a much more widespread sport towards the end of the century. However many of the people who worked on the land could not take part because there were laws which prevented them.
4. Horse-racing too was developing. Nevertheless it was so poorly organised that there were no regular programmes of events and there were few rules.
5. Lawn tennis grew in popularity. All the same it was readily available only to those who were allowed to play on lawns in the richer parts of cities.
6. Today boxing is fought under strict rules and boxers wear padded gloves, whereas last century the contestants fought with bare fists and went on fighting until one man was unable to stand up any longer.
7. The type of cricket that was played in the mid-nineteenth century was fairly similar to modern cricket although players bowled underarm and used curved bats and some of them wore top hats and boots.
8. In the first half of the century football players were allowed to knock the ball down with their hands as well as kick it, but in the 1860s football split into two games, rugby and soccer.

Order of Events

The writer also uses clue words to show the order in which events happened (as well as to connect his statements).

Example
As soon as Mr Edwards read about Bill Jamieson's record run in his car, he decided to set up his own record by car from his home to the city.
Two events are mentioned: (a) Mr Edwards read about Bill's record.
(b) Mr Edwards decided to make his own record.
Which happened first, (a) or (b)? The answer is (a). The words that give us the clue are *as soon as*.

A For each paragraph (1–9) decide whether (a) or (b) happened first and write out the clue words which tell you.

Nineteenth-century record attempt

1. Before Mr Edwards set out on his journey, he had asked the chemist in Bygate to have 15 litres of petrol ready for the second half of the journey.
   - (a) he ordered petrol
   - (b) he set out

   (*Answer* (*a*) happened first. Clue word: *before*)

2. He was almost stunned when he heard how much the chemist charged for petrol.
   - (a) he was surprised
   - (b) he heard the price of petrol

3. It was only after his stop at Alven that he realised the radiator water had boiled away.
   - (a) he stopped at Alven
   - (b) he realised the radiator was dry

4. A series of strange vibrations soon after he set out again began to worry him.
   - (a) the car began to vibrate
   - (b) he set off again

5. As soon as he managed to pull off the main road, he ran to the nearest blacksmith to ask for help.
   - (a) he pulled off the main road
   - (b) he ran to the blacksmith

6. The car was not ready for the next part of the journey until the blacksmith had worked for many hours.
   - (a) the car was ready
   - (b) the blacksmith worked for many hours

7. The next major delay occurred after the tyre on the nearside rear wheel came off.
   - (a) there was a major delay
   - (b) the tyre came off

8. Brake failure nearly caused a disaster as he descended Beard Hill Road. Immediately Mr Edwards decided to abandon his record attempt.
   - (a) the brakes failed
   - (b) Mr Edwards decided to give up

9. It was a sad and disappointed Mr Edwards who returned home. Thereafter he intimated that he would take no further part in attempting any records in his car.
   - (a) Mr Edwards returned home
   - (b) he said he would make no further record attempts

Bicycles in Britain

B Below are five paragraphs (a), (b), (c), (d) and (e). They are written out in the wrong order. Read them carefully and look for clues to the correct order. Write (a) to (e) in the right order.

(a) More than fifty years later along came the boneshaker. It had wooden wheels with iron hoops and it had pedals fixed to the front wheel.

(b) Three years later in 1888 Dunlop produced air-filled tyres for bicycles. This made cycling more comfortable and much safer.

(c) The first bicycle appeared in England over one hundred and seventy years ago. It was known as the *hobby horse* and had been invented in France. The rider had to swing his legs and as his toes touched the ground, he pushed himself along.

(d) From then on there have been gradual improvements right up to the modern bicycle of the type such as you yourself may have.

(e) The Rover Safety Bicycle, built in Coventry in 1885, was a big step forward. At last we had something like a modern bicycle. The wheels were of the same size and it was driven by pedals connected by a chain to the rear hub.

C What would be the correct order of the pictures 1, 2, 3, 4 and 5?

first: No. 3

69

Joining Sentences

A In the passage below there are too many short sentences which are not linked well together. Rewrite the passage. Wherever you see a dash – join the preceding sentence and the one following into a longer sentence. You may on some occasions use conjunctions (eg. *and, but, although*, etc.), or you may use relative pronouns (eg. *which, who, that*). In some cases you may wish to re-arrange the order of words, leave out some words or put in some new words. You might begin the second paragraph:

> *This is the huge lion with a human head* . . .

What picture does the word *Egypt* conjure up in your mind? The River Nile, Cairo, deserts and pyramids perhaps. In one day in Egypt you could visit them all and also the Sphinx which stands in close proximity to the Great Pyramid.

This is the huge lion. – It has a human head. – It has been sculptured out of limestone rock. It is about seventy-three metres long. – It towers in excess of eighteen metres in height from the base to the top of its head.

How long will this great monument stand guard beside the Pyramids? It has done well to survive thousands of years. – One considers the dangers to its existence over such a long time.

This part of Egypt is too far away from the Nile to benefit from its floodwaters. There is always a carpet of sand. – This in itself would be relatively harmless. – In combination with strong winds it regularly launches its attack on the monument. Sandstorms certainly do not improve the structure. – On occasions they can threaten to bury it. Sometimes it has been necessary to dig it out. – It might have disappeared beneath the sand, possibly for ever.

The extremes of temperature have had their effect too. Egyptian day-time temperatures are intense during parts of the year. – Balanced against that are the low temperatures at night and at certain other times of the year. The effect of the sheer intensity of the heat and subsequent cooling must affect the rock as time passes.

Air pollution is a hazard of recent origin. The motor car is used extensively in nearby Cairo. – In that city there are many traffic jams. This leads to a build-up of exhaust fumes. – The fumes pollute the air. Polluted air is carried on to the Sphinx stone work. – Slowly and imperceptibly damage is done to the human-headed lion of rock.

Another recent problem is the presence of underground water near the base of the monument. This was discovered in 1978 by an American research team. – Their report indicated that water was seeping up into the porous limestone rock. As the water evaporates it leaves its crystals of salt. – They are making the stone so brittle that it breaks away.

But why should there be any water in the desert area? The explanation seems to lie in the village of Nazlet-el-Samman. – It has no sewage system. There is a maze of underground passages in the area. – Sewage has been flowing into them. Those have now become clogged up with water. – It should have been drained away by proper sewage pipes.

All these factors do their worst to the Sphinx. – It deteriorates as time goes on. Recently a leg fell off. It had been built of stone blocks by people who had done restoration work centuries ago.

Archaeologists naturally worry. – They wish to see it preserved. Just for comparatively short-term repairs half a million pounds would be required. Major repairs and restoration are also required. – Vast additional sums are needed.

For Egypt it is a problem. – She does not have the finance to spare. Visitors bring in money to the country. – They will come and spend it only if the Sphinx and other sights are there to attract them. How is she to spend money she does not have so that she can attract tourists who will bring in the money she needs?

Assignment

Choose a piece of text in which the writer uses a number of connecting expressions like those on pages 64–7. (You may find useful material in biography, history, news and sports reports.) If it is from a source which will be thrown away, like a newspaper, blot out all the connecting words and phrases, and see how successfully your friend can fill them in.

If your text is from a more permanent source, you will need to copy it out, leaving blanks in place of the linking expressions.

8. Point of View

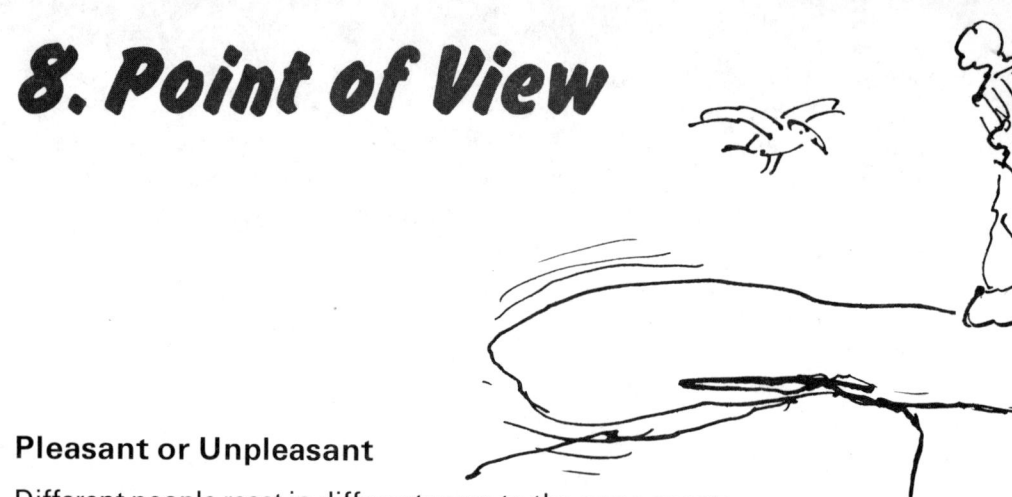

Pleasant or Unpleasant

Different people react in different ways to the same events, information or ideas.

Passages A and B (pages 72–3) show how differently children reacted to wartime evacuation.

A 1. Write down five happy experiences mentioned in A.
2. Write down five unhappy experiences mentioned in B.
3. What did you notice when you compared how the Graham children and the Edwards children felt about
    (a) their new schools
    (b) their homes?
4. If a reporter had published passage A, what would he be hoping to make his readers think?
5. If another reporter had published passage B, what would he be hoping his readers would think?

A

Mr and Mrs Edwards had four children, Anna, Ella, James and Tom. All their lives they had lived in the city and rarely had been outside it. They were happy in their home and had no desire to leave it.

But when war broke out, Mrs Edwards took the children away to live in a country cottage about 32 km away. Mr Edwards came out to see them at weekends and during the evenings when he did not have to work late.

The children loved the new experience. The open spaces and the clean fresh air were a delight. They roamed over the fields and hills, they played in safety far away from busy traffic, and they were often allowed to help a Mr Williams. He was so short of workers that he was pleased to have their assistance.

The new school was quiet and different but in its own way it was exciting and enjoyable. They were in small classes in the little school and soon they had made friends with everyone there. The long walk to school was something very novel at first. All city children seemed to have their schools very near at hand.

There were no street lights in the village but the lights in the towns were all blacked out anyway. In the cottage there was no electric light but their oil lamps burned bright and cheerful, and the coal stove cooked their food as well as any gas fire. The children hoped their stay would be a long one.

B

The excitement in the Graham family grew to fever pitch in the last few days before the war. It had been decided to evacuate the children from the centre of the city. The destination of the Graham children was to be a village some twenty kilometres out in the country. Mrs Graham and the children set out on their new adventure two days before the declaration of war.

Within a week the excitement was over. Jane, Maurice and Tom felt so lonely far away from their home and their friends. In place of the hustle and bustle of the town and the great throngs of people always on the move, in the village there seemed to be nothing. Just plain nothing. No people, or hardly any, no traffic, and not a shop worthy of the name.

At school the local children looked at them as if they were oddities to be laughed at every time they spoke in their city accents. There were so few children to play with. The teacher did not seem to like them. They were told to do the same work as the rest of the class. Some of it they had done before and some was far too difficult. They longed to be back at their own school with their own friends and teacher. But a letter from Jane's friend informed them that there was hardly anyone left there now.

The afternoons and evenings after the school day were particularly dull. There seemed to be so little to do that was either interesting or exciting. Their new house was far too quiet. It was to them a strange kind of house, with no gas, or electricity or radio. Maurice even said he would prefer to be bombed in town rather than live out so unhappy a life in the country.

For or Against

A The following passage shows the different attitudes of three people towards the idea of Donovan coming to stay. Read the passage carefully before answering the following questions.

   Which one is (a) very much in favour
               (b) rather unconcerned
               (c) not in favour?

   In each case ((a), (b), and (c)) give evidence from the passage to support your answer.

For Keith, though, it had been a decision of his parents and that was that. It'd probably work out. No good worrying too much. But it would be strange actually having a black boy living indoors. He got on well with most of the black kids at school, but having one at home all the time would be bound to be a bit different.

Keith's mother must have felt the same because she couldn't quite settle to anything while Keith was taking the message to school until she had explained it all to Mrs Parsons next door. She didn't want the boy to arrive in the car without the ground being prepared. Mrs Parsons could be quite put out over some·things.

Keith let himself in through the front door just as his mother got to the crux of things over a low part of the fence at the back. Mrs Parsons, a short, thin woman, just too old in Mr Chapman's opinion for the mini-skirts she wore, was pegging out an apricot coloured nightie and one sock.

"Yes, he's a dear little boy from a West Indian family," said Mrs Chapman.

"Oh," said Mrs Parsons, a bit straight. "I know there's a lot about," as if she were talking about an illness. "Why's he coming all this way to you?"

Mrs Chapman realized that she had given the wrong impression about Donovan.

"Well, he's not coming so far," she replied, "only from North London. His father works there in a factory. Now his mother has been called back to nurse her father in Jamaica, and the authorities say Donovan's father can't look after him properly on his own. He works such long hours. So Donovan's being fostered by us until his mother comes back."

"Oh, I see," said Mrs Parsons. "Very nice for them too, I suppose. Just up and leave the children and we have to pay out to have them looked after." She made it sound as if Mrs Chapman were making a gigantic profit out of some personal welfare service provided by Mr and Mrs Parsons. She began to stuff some spare pegs into her skirt pocket, ready to go indoors.

"It's not quite as bad as it seems," Mrs Chapman put in quickly. "The father's paying for his keep. But even if he wasn't, they've lived here for twelve years, and Donovan was born here. So really he's as British as you and I."

Mrs Parsons looked offended.

"Besides, his parents pay rates and taxes just like us, so they're entitled to some of the benefits when they need them. And I'm sure you wouldn't like to see a little boy left to roam the streets in all weathers till his dad comes home at eight o'clock. You wouldn't have liked that for your Ronnie."

She drew a breath, surprised at her own flow of words.

"Yes, well that's true, I suppose," said Mrs Parsons,

definitely going in now. "But things have changed a lot since I moved in here." She bent awkwardly to pick up a fallen peg on the way. "And not all for the better."

Mrs Chapman sighed and turned away. Mrs Parsons had taken the news much as she had feared, and things weren't going to be all sweetness and light between the neighbours for the next few months, that was clear. However, she was not the sort of person to be put off a thing by somebody's stupid attitude. She hurried into the house. There were things to be done. A dinner to cook, a bed to make up and a room to prepare for Donovan.

"Come on, give us a hand," she said to Keith.

(Ashley *The Trouble with Donovan Croft*)

Selecting Facts

Writers often show their point of view by selecting only those facts that support what they think.

1. Compare the first paragraph in A (page 75) with the first paragraph in B (page 76). Each paragraph agrees that bombing of cities increased.
   Write down another item on which the first paragraphs agree.
2. Compare the second paragraph in A with the second paragraph in B.
   Write down one item on which the paragraphs agree.
3. First paragraph in A and first paragraph in B disagree about the fear that affected people in cities.
   Study the second paragraphs and write down one item on which they disagree.
4. Study the third paragraphs and write down one item on which the writers would disagree.
5. Write out and complete the following sentences after you have studied A and B.
   (a) The writer of A sets out to show
   (b) The writer of B sets out to show

A

1. As more and more heavy bombing raids were directed against the cities of Great Britain, ordinary men and women showed great courage. Night after night many sought refuge in air raid shelters and underground railway shelters. With little complaint they suffered many discomforts and hardships, but they refused to give way to fear or despair. In fact they kept up remarkably cheerful spirits.
2. The government saw to it that during times of shortage

important things such as food, clothes and petrol were shared out. To achieve this they introduced rationing. People realised the advantages when they saw that all could get what they were entitled to. And each person was willing to share in making the sacrifices that were necessary.

3. There was also evidence of a new willingness amongst ordinary people to work together. They were eager to help each other. Strangers would help strangers for all knew they were striving to defeat the common enemy.

4. In spite of all the inconveniences and suffering of the war years, people went about their work with a will and enthusiasm that had not been seen for years. On the farms, in the factories, in the mines and in the shops and offices everyone showed what could be done when people were determined to win.

B

1. When fears of direct invasion became less, the bombing of British cities increased. In parts of Britain defenceless men and women were subjected to the almost nightly attacks. The German bombs struck fear and terror in those who huddled together in air raid shelters and underground stations. The fact that they did not complain as much as one might have expected did not mean that sufferings were not severe.

2. Although parliament brought in restrictions, such as rationing, to try to make sure that all did have enough food and clothes, etc., many did not obey the restrictions as might have been expected at a time of crisis. Some were able to get much more than their fair shares whilst others, especially those with little money, had to make do with much less.

3. It would be pointless to pretend that all citizens helped each other as has been suggested by some writers. The crimes of peacetime still continued. During the black out theft and robbery went on. This was regrettable when all should have been working together to win the war.

4. Workers in the factories, farms and mines all had plenty of work because many of their colleagues were away serving in the armed services. But the will to win did not stop strikes during the war years. On occasions workers felt their grievances were so severe that they stopped work until they were settled, even though the nation was at war and could ill afford to lose working days.

Selecting Arguments

A   Writers and speakers will select arguments to suit their case.
Look at the articles on page 78.

1. Write in a few words each main argument used by A for raising the price. One has been given for you.
   (a) supplies will run out
   (b), (c), (d)
2. Write in a few words each main argument used by B for reducing the price. One has been given for you.
   (a) Britain has more than enough
   (b), (c), (d)
3. Which group of people would be likely to use the arguments in A?
4. Which people might use the arguments in B?
5. Write out in your own words a balanced (unbiased) statement which combines the arguments in A and B about (a) supply, (b) price, and (c) saving of fuel. To do this complete each of the following:
   (a) *Supply of fuel*
       Britain has abundant supplies of gas and oil at the moment, but . . . .
   (b) *Price of fuel*
       An increase in price would result in a saving of fuel, but . . . .
   (c) *Saving of fuel*
       Measures being taken to save fuel will mean that it will not run out as quickly as it will at the present rate of use, but . . . .

A

Fuel prices should rise

Britain's sources of gas and oil will not last for ever. By the end of the twentieth century there may be shortages of both.

It is time to begin to conserve our supplies now. At the moment far too much fuel is wasted in both homes and factories.

There are studies already in hand to achieve savings in fuel such as loft and cavity wall insulation in houses, installation of more efficient machines in factories, and development of car engines which use less fuel. But such schemes are not adequate to solve the problem.

The only real solution is to increase the price. If fuel was much dearer than it is at present, people would use it more carefully and sparingly.

The increase in price would not cause much hardship. People would use less and what they cut out would be the present waste. And once they have eliminated waste, the new fuel bills will not be much higher than they are at present.

Prices must rise NOW.

B

Fuel prices must fall

Britain is a country rich in oil and gas. So plentiful is oil that it is sold abroad in large quantities.

It is utterly unacceptable that prices should be so high. It is a generally accepted principle that when things are in plentiful supply they are cheap. Only when they become scarce can high prices be justified.

Fuel is a basic necessity in every home for heating and lighting and operating all the modern gadgets. To keep prices high is to make the cost of living high for everyone.

The argument that supplies of existing fuels will eventually run out is no excuse. By that time undoubtedly plenty of alternative supplies of fuel will have been discovered and perhaps they will be very cheap. One hopes that electricity produced by waves of the sea will be just one such example.

So let us have cheap fuel NOW.

Which Opinion?

The following extracts are taken from the *Radio Times* and from a daily newspaper. Both deal with the same three programmes. Read them then answer the questions on page 80.

BBC1

7.40 pm
The Saturday Film:
Escape from Zahrain

starring
Yul Brynner as Sharif
Sal Mineo as Ahmed
James Mason as Johnson
Madlyn Rhue as Laila
Jack Warden as Huston
Tony Caruso as Tahar
Jay Novello as Hassan
Escaping from prison in a strife-torn Arab State, a strange convoy of desperate men take a girl hostage and flee across the desert towards the frontier. Yul Brynner stars as a dedicated nationalist leader in this colourful and explosive adventure.

BBC2

7.40 pm
The Chess Players

starring **Richard Attenborough, Amjad Khan, Sanjeev Kumar, Saeed Jaffrey**
BBC2 concludes its contribution to the Festival of India with Satyajit Ray's first historical film. It is a delicate and compassionate treatment of the annexation of the state of Oudh by the British. Counterpointing this inglorious incident is the continuing duel of the two chess-playing noblemen, sublimely oblivious of political and private turmoil in their obsession for the game.

Mirza Sajjd Ali........... SANJEEV KUMAR
Meer Roshan Ali.........SAEED JAFFREY
King Wajid Ali ....AMJAD KHAN
General Outram
              RICHARD ATTENBOROUGH
Khurshid .... SHABANA AZMI
Nafeesa ....FARIDA JALAL
Aulea Begum, Wajid's mother ... VEENA
Munshi Nandial .... DAVID ABRAHAM
Ali Naqi Khan, Prime Minister of Oudh
              VICTOR BANNERJI
Aqil......................FAROOQUE SHAIKH
Captain Weston................ TOM ALTER
Hiria .... LEELA MISHRA
Dr Joseph Fayrer ....BARRY JOHN

Screenplay by SATYAJIT RAY
based on the story by MUNSHI PREMCHAND
Directed by SATYAJIT RAY. *Films: page 15*
A Hindi film with English subtitles

12.5-1.25 am
Midnight Movie:
Poison Pen

continues the short series of
Flora Robson films
Also starring
Robert Newton, Ann Todd
Dame Flora Robson stars as the lonely and embittered sister of a vicar in this tale of suspicion and scandal in an English village. The peaceful life of Hilldale is shattered as villagers begin to receive vicious poison-pen letters accusing them of misdemeanours. Rumours and hatred lead to tragedy before a handwriting expert steps in.

Mary Rider................. FLORA ROBSON
Sam Hurrin .... ROBERT NEWTON
Ann Rider .... ANN TODD
David.................... GEOFFREY TOONE
The Rev Rider .... REGINALD TATE
Sucal Hurrin .... BELLE CHRYSTAL
Len Griffin .... EDWARD CHAPMAN
Badham.................... EDWARD RIGBY
Col Casbelton .... ATHOLE STEWART
Mrs Casbelton ....MARY HINTON
Peter Casbelton.... CYRIL CHAMBERLAIN

Screenplay by
DOREEN MONTGOMERY, WILLIAM FRESHMAN, W. C. HUNTER, ESTHER MCCRACKEN
Produced by WALTER C. MYCROFT
Directed by PAUL STEIN
(First showing on British television)
(Black and white). Films: page 15
(Saraband for Dead Lovers: Mon 3:35)

Newspaper 27-3-82
Weekend television and radio

7.40 Film: Escape from Zahrain (1962). One you might want to escape from – a bit of a yawn as Yul Brynner leads an escape across the desert from a troubled Arab state. Photography quite good. Sal Mineo, Madlyn Rhue and Jack Warden also star, with James Mason away down the cast.

7.40 Film: The Chess Players (1977). In deference to the Festival of India, a showing of this interesting film starring Richard Attenborough and Saeed Jaffrey in the story of the annexation by the British of an Indian state in 1856. Hindi with English sub-titles.

12.5 Film: Poison Pen (1939). Average drama about a village community in conflict over vindictive anonymous letters. Fine performance from Flora Robson, with Robert Newton and Ann Todd co-starring (black and white).

1. Which phrase is used in the *Radio Times* to make "Escape from Zahrain" sound attractive?
2. What does the newspaper think of "Escape from Zahrain"?
3. *Radio Times* states that there is "delicate and compassionate" treatment of the subject in "Chess Players". How does the newspaper describe the film?
4. What kind of film does the *Radio Times* seem to suggest "Poison Pen" is?
5. What does the newspaper think of "Poison Pen"?
6. Why would you expect the *Radio Times* to make all three sound attractive?
7. The newspaper is no doubt trying to give readers unbiased comments. But why might you not accept without question what the newspaper says?

Assignments

1. Work in a group of four or more. Each member of the group should bring in a newspaper of the same date – collect as many different papers as you can. In each newspaper, study two of the following items and pick out examples of different points of view in the different papers:
   opinion column
   letters to the Editor
   television/film reviews
   sports reports
   political reports
2. Compare and contrast the same story in two newspapers.